TS-166

Keeping and Breeding
GECKOS

Hermann Seufer

An Hawequa Thick-toed Gecko,
Afroedura hawequensis. Photo by
John Visser.

New Zealand Green Gecko, *Naultinus elegans*, female. Photo by K. H. Switak.

Keeping and Breeding
GECKOS

Hermann Seufer

Keeping and Breeding
GECKOS
HERMANN SEUFER

1995 Edition

Geckos have a justifiable claim to the title of "Most Unusual Lizards." Not only are they gorgeous colors, personable, and often easy to maintain in captivity, but they breed well, eat cockroaches, and even bark during the night! With the recent increase in availability of captive-bred geckos of many species, geckos have become a major force in the terrarium hobby and are still gaining strength as more and more colorful species become known to hobbyists.

Because they are such new pets, there is little information on gecko husbandry available for the average hobbyist. Keeping and Breeding Geckos is the first modern coverage of the principal species of the group that are being kept and bred today. The species are discussed extensively, with emphasis on successfully breeding each species and rearing the young. Although small, geckos can be long-lived, successful, and very productive pets for the terrarium hobbyist.

CONTENTS

Gekko gecko, the Tokay. Photo by Burkhard Kahl.

FOREWORD

For generations, man has been impressed by the behavior of geckos, lizards of the family Gekkonidae. Many tall tales involving geckos have survived to this day. In the last few years interest in keeping this group of lizards in terraria has steadily increased. At first mainly species from Europe, North Africa, and the Near East were kept, but, with the advent of fast and reliable transport, geckos from the most remote corners of the earth have become available. They are easy to keep (with a few exceptions) at relatively low expense, have interesting behavior, and many have attractive patterns or colors. These attributes make them ideal subjects for the terrarium. With careful husbandry, many species will breed successfully in captivity, so gecko keepers in the future will not have to rely wholly on wild-caught specimens. Many species of nocturnal geckos and some of the day geckos of the genus *Phelsuma* are already being bred in sufficient numbers to supply the terrarium market.

Although geckos have been kept in terraria for many decades, to date there has been little reference material available on husbandry and breeding. This is a problem not only to the beginner, but also to the experienced keeper who acquires a new species. As a keeper of geckos for many years I also found information difficult to obtain, so with this book I am attempting to fill the information gap. Another aspect that persuaded me to write this work was that many books and papers described geckos as a relatively uniform family of lizards. This is definitely not the case. With the geckos, we are dealing with a great variety of forms that have colonized the most diverse ecological niches, as I hope to show in the following text.

In the descriptions of species, I have chosen to include those species that are readily available on the market plus others of which breeding groups are held by enthusiasts. As well as drawing from my own experiences and observations, those of other gecko experts have been included, in particular the eminent gecko breeder E. Schroeder of Kiel, who has unselfishly given me much valuable information, and to whom I am greatly indebted. My thanks also go to all those unnamed gecko keepers who during many conversations have helped me to make up deficiencies in information. For the critical reading of the manuscript and for supplying me with much appropriate literature during the whole time I have kept geckos, I must offer my heartfelt thanks to Herr Dr. W. Boehme of Bonn. Any errors of fact or observation are, of course, mine.

INTRODUCING GECKOS

The geckos (Gekkonidae), the snake-like flap-footed or scaley-footed lizards (Pygopodidae), and the night lizards (Xantusiidae) form the infraorder of gecko-like lizards (Gekkota). While there are several obvious anatomical similarities between the geckos and the flap-foots, similarities to the skink-like (Scincomorpha) night lizards are not so obvious.

Geckos have existed on earth for at least 50 million years. They probably arose from ardeosaurs or their immediate ancestors in the Jurassic period. A complete picture of gecko evolution is not possible, as the earliest fossil geckos are known only from the Eocene (some 50-60 million years ago). They must have already been worldwide in distribution at this time, and they probably had already begun to fill diverse ecological niches.

Geckos originated in Southeast Asia (where today *Aeluroscalabotes*, the most primitive gecko genus, still lives) and radiated out to many parts

Cyrtodactylus pulchellus, often called the Malayan Jewel Gecko. Photo by Kenneth T. Nemuras.

of the earth. Since the 14th and 15th centuries and the increase in sea transport, man has played a part in the dispersion of these creatures. In particular, geckos of the genus *Hemidactylus* have, by means of ships, colonized many parts of the earth other than their original habitat. Today geckos are found on the continents and many islands between latitudes 50° North and 50° South.

In this large area they have colonized the most diverse of habitats. They range from sea-level to altitudes of 4000 m (13,000 ft). The leaf-fingered gecko *Phyllodactylus angustidigitatus* of Peru lives directly in the tidal zone and even takes refuge in the sea. The European Leaf-fingered Gecko, *Phyllodactylus europaeus*, has also been found close to the sea. In Morocco, the Atlas Day Gecko, *Quedenfeldia trachyblepharus*, is found from sea-level to 4000 m. In addition to these examples of tidal zones and mountains, gecko species have also acclimated to arid (steppe, desert, etc.) and wet (rain forest) areas. Many species have taken to human habitations and other buildings. Geckos have only been able to colonize these various habitats through their different physical attributes (the development of adhesive toes, fat-storing tails, etc.) and the evolution of certain behaviors (for example, night activity).

Geckos are small (under 40

Artist's reconstruction of the giant gecko *Hoplodactylus delacourti*, perhaps extinct. Art by John R. Quinn.

mm, 1.5 in) to medium sized (37 cm, 14.5 in) lizards that always have well developed limbs. The maximum length (62 cm, over 2 feet) is based on *Hoplodactylus delacourti*, a single stuffed specimen of unknown origin and probably extinct. Otherwise, most other living geckos are under 25 cm (10 inches) in length.

The gecko family contains some 800 living species split into four subfamilies:

Eublepharinae (Eyelid Geckos)
Diplodactylinae (Double-fingered Geckos)
Gekkoninae (Typical Geckos)
Sphaerodactylinae (Sphere-fingered Geckos)

The Genera of Geckos

Although admittedly incomplete, the following listing of gecko genera and number of included species is presented for ease of reference if a strange name should appear and you would like to make sure it is a gecko. The taxonomy of geckos is unsettled at the moment, with new genera and species still being described, old genera being merged with others, and new genera being formed by breaking up other genera.

Aeluroscalabotes (2)
Afroedura (6)
Agamura (3)
Ailuronyx (2)
Alsophylax (8)
Anarbylus (1)
Ancylodactylus (1)
Aristelliger (6)
Asaccus (2)
Bavayia (2)
Bogertia (1)
Briba (1)
Bunopus (5)
Calodactylus (2)
Carphodactylus (1)
Chondrodactylus (1)
Cnemaspis (24)
Coleodactylus (4)
Coleonyx (5)

Colopus (1)
Cosymbotus (2)
Crenadactylus (1)
Crossobamon (4)
Cyrtodactylus (70)
Diplodactylus (25)
Dravidogecko (1)
Ebenavia (1)
Eublepharis (6)
Eurydactylodes (2)
Garthia (1)
Geckolepis (5)
Geckonia (1)
Gehyra (22)
Geopristurus (1)
Gekko (20)
Gonatodes (20)
Gymnodactylus (1)
Hemidactylus (70)
Hemiphyllodactylus (2)
Hemitheconyx (2)
Heteronotia (2)
Heteropholis (6)
Holodactylus (2)
Homonota (10)
Homopholis (3)
Hoplodactylus (4)
Kaokogecko (1)
Lepidoblepharis (8)
Lepidodactylus (15)
Lucasium (1)
Luperosaurus (3)
Lygodactylus (50)
Microscalabotes (1)
Millotisaurus (1)
Narudasia (1)
Naultinus (2)
Nephrurus (6)
Oedura (10)
Pachydactylus (30)
Padydactylus (1)
Palmatogecko (1)
Paragehyra (1)
Paroedura (8)
Perochirus (3)
Phelsuma (25)

Two of the most snake-like pygopodids or scaley-foots, *Pygopus nigriceps*, above, and *Pygopus lepidopodus*, below, both from Australia. Photos by K. H. Switak.

Phyllodactylus (70)
Phyllopezus (1)
Phyllurus (6)
Pristurus (8)
Pseudogekko (5)
Pseudogonatodes (5)
Pseudothecadactylus (2)
Ptenopus (3)
Ptychozoon (5)
Ptyodactylus (2)
Quedenfeldtia (1)
Rhacodactylus (6)
Rhoptropella (1)
Rhoptropus (7)
Rhynchoedura (1)
Saurodactylus (2)
Sphaerodactylus (85)
Stenodactylus (12)
Tarentola (8)
Teratolepis (2)
Teratoscincus (4)
Thecadactylus (1)
Trachydactylus (8)
Tropidocalotes (4)
Underwoodisaurus (2)
Uroplatus (6)
Wallsaurus (2)

The Scalation

The body of these slender but strongly built lizards is covered with small, flat (but sometimes lightly keeled) granular scales that give the skin a soft and silken appearance. In many species large single- or multi-keeled tubercular scales are situated between the granular scales on the upper sides of the limbs, on the back, and on the upper side of the tail. On the tail especially, the tubercles are often thorn-like. On the back they may be distributed randomly or arranged in obvious rows.

Members of the genera *Geckolepis* and *Teratoscincus* have developed a variation on the typical gecko skin form. In

The Thick-tailed Gecko, *Underwoodisaurus milii*, from near Sydney, Australia. Photo by K. H. Switak.

An adult *Sphaerodactylus elegans*. Photo by Robert S. Simmons.

these genera, the back, the belly, the tail, and parts of the limbs are covered with large, flat scales arranged similarly as those on a fish. These scales are not strongly attached to the underlying skin and may be shed in large patches if the reptiles are molested. Apart from protection (passive defense) for the animal, which works in much the same way as tail autotomy (voluntary shedding), these scales are connected with gas exchange through dermal respiration in *Teratoscincus scincus*. The development of these "fish scales" can be conveniently studied in the genus *Teratoscincus*. While *T. microlepis* has only small, barely overlapping scales, those of the two species *T. scincus* and *T. bedriagai* are highly developed.

Like all scaled reptiles, geckos must shed their outer skin (the epidermis) at regular intervals. In the Helmeted Gecko, *Geckonia chazaliae*, the skin has been observed to loosen at particular points (the toes, the flanks, and the snout). Many geckos actively aid shedding by tearing particles of loose skin from the toes and the tail with their mouths. Some geckos devour all of their shed skin, some part of it, and others none of it. There is no exact data available on the shedding cycles of the various species, but it is suspected that the quality of the

When most geckos shed, the skin tends to break into large and small pieces that may be eaten. Above is a shedding *Coleonyx variegatus*, the Banded Desert Gecko, and below is a shedding *Cyrtodactylus pulchellus*. Photo above by Alex Kerstitch, that below by Kenneth T. Nemuras.

In some geckos the skin comes off mostly in one large piece that looks a bit like the shed skin of a tiny snake. This *Pachydactylus bibroni* seems to be casting an almost complete shed. Photo by John Visser.

Above: *Teratoscincus microlepis*, a wonder gecko with fine scales. Photo by Robert S. Simmons. Below: The squat Helmeted Gecko, *Geckonia chazaliae*. Photo by R. D. Bartlett.

Phelsuma madagascariensis, one of the most attractive of the day geckos. Notice the round pupil found in only a few groups of diurnal (day-active) geckos. Photo by H. Hansen.

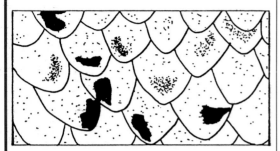

Detail of the scales of the Wonder Gecko, *Teratoscincus scincus*. These smooth, plain scales overlap each other fairly uniformly.

diet, in particular the availability of vitamin D$_3$, plays a part. During shedding, it is wise to keep a close watch on your geckos and ensure that the casting of the skin is complete, particularly on the toes and the

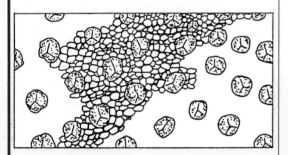

Detail of the scales of the Sand Gecko, *Chondrodactylus angulifer*, showing the smooth, granulated scales strewn with large keeled scales.

tail tip. If parts of the old skin remain on these extremities for any length of time, there is a danger of the part dying. To prevent this, be sure that there is a slightly damp spot in the terrarium where the animals will spend some time before shedding. When the skin lightens in color and the animal appears to be about to shed,

increase the fine mist spraying. If pieces of unshed skin persist, do not hesitate to remove them, as they will otherwise soon harden. The skin can be softened with lukewarm water and gently peeled away. For geckos without adhesive lamellae, the skin of the toes can be softened with a little cod-liver oil.

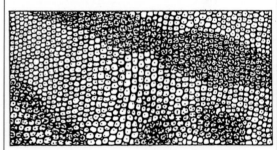

Detail of the scalation of the the Banded Desert Gecko, *Coleonyx variegatus*, showing the uniform smooth, granular scales.

Toes and Tails

Apart from a few scalation characteristics such as pointed supraocular scales (ciliate scales) and spine-like tail scales (*Diplodactylus ciliaris*), the structure of the fingers and toes is of particular importance in gecko identification. Many scientific and common names of geckos are related to the form of the digits, for example: *Cyrtodactylus* (bow-finger); *Gymnodactylus* (naked-finger); *Phyllodactylus* (leaf-finger); *Saurodactylus* (lizard-finger).

More than two-thirds of the 800 or so species of modern geckos have developed adhesive lamellae on their digits, while

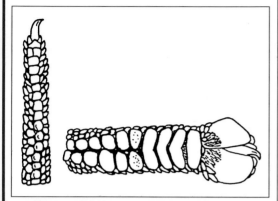

Undersides of the toes of *Eublepharis kuroiwae* (left), lacking lamellae, and *Diplodactylus ciliaris* (right), with large lamellae and pads below the claw.

Foot of the Turnip-tail, *Thecadactylus rapicauda*, showing the double row of lamellae. Photo by Kenneth T. Nemuras.

the remainder have either never developed them or have lost them through further evolution (like the South African *Chondrodactylus angulifer*). In sandy areas where there are few opportunities to climb, geckos have not developed adhesive pads on their digits, but other adaptations may be present. The Web-footed Gecko, *Palmatogecko rangei*, has "webbed" toes that enable it to quickly "swim" into the sand to escape predators. Similarly, *Stenodactylus* (thin-fingered) and *Teratoscincus* species have comb-like projections on their toes. Among the many species with adhesive toe-pads, there is great variety. The climbing ability of the sphere-fingered geckos *(Sphaerodactylus)* relies on a single spherical pad at each toe-

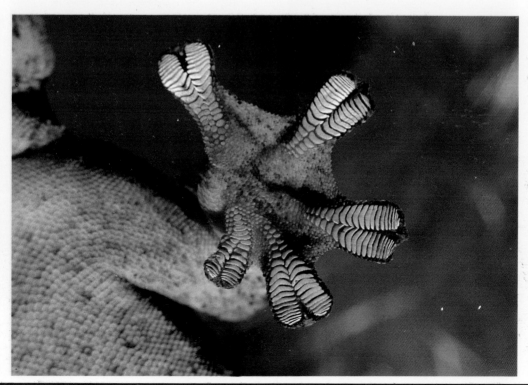

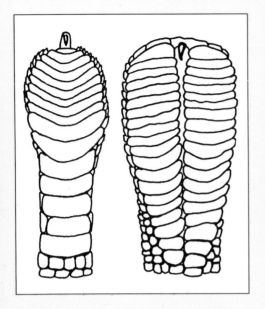

Above: Undersides of the toes of *Ptychozoon lionatum* (left), with a single row of lamellae, and *Thecadactylus rapicauda* (right), with a double row. Below: *Hemidactylus mabouia*, showing the large claws of the toes. Photo by Kenneth T. Nemuras.

tip. The leaf-fingered geckos (*Phyllodactylus*) have two subdigital pads under each digit, plus a claw. In the genera *Tarentola* and *Gekko* each digit is noticeably widened by a broad row of lamellae. The *Hemidactylus* species and the Turnip-tail *(Thecadactylus rapicauda)* have two rows of lamellae on each digit. In spite of the different forms of adhesive pads, their structure and function are similar.

Each single lamella is furnished with numerous tiny, hair-like bristles that are referred to as setae. Each seta has a number of microscopic flat-ended branches known as spatulae. The tiny spatulae are thought to act as little suction cups. Depending on the species,

each seta has between 100 and 1000 such spatulae. Impressive numbers indeed!

In addition to the suction cup theory, there is another school of thought that suggests that static electricity plays a part in giving the lamellae adhesive powers. Whatever causes it to work, it is so efficient that even dead geckos will adhere to surfaces.

In addition to adhesive pads, most species possess well developed claws as additional aids to climbing. Some species are able to withdraw their claws into little pouches or sheaths.

Gecko tails have almost as many variations as the digits. In some species the tail has developed quite definite functions. The wide tail of the Leopard Gecko is used as fat-

Ptychozoon kuhli, a flying gecko. Photo by Ken Lucas, Steinhart Aquarium.

storage. The Australian species *Diplodactylus conspicillatus* uses its tail to block its burrow. To startle predators, *Teratoscincus scincus* can make sounds similar to the chirruping of a cricket by

From underneath, the gliding fringe and various other skin flaps are visible on this *Ptychozoon kuhli*. Photo by Ken Lucas, Steinhart Aquarium,

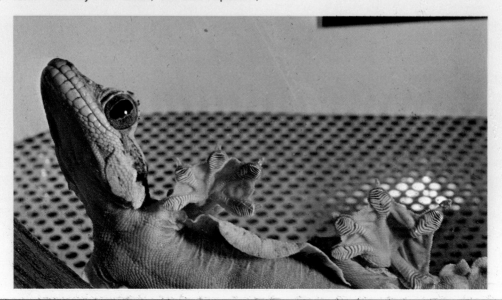

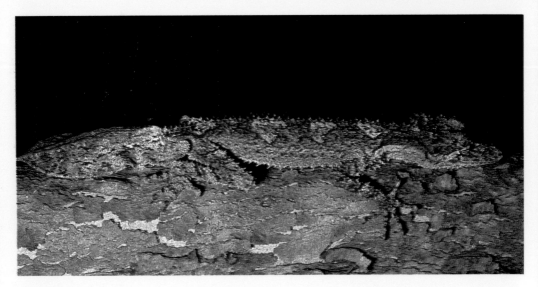

Phyllurus cornutus, the Northern Leaf-tailed Gecko of Australia. Perfect camouflage against bark. Photo by K. H. Switak.

movements of the tail scales. Members of the genera *Lygodactylus, Phyllodactylus* (some Old-World species only), *Phelsuma,* and *Rhacodactylus* have adhesive or prehensile tails.

Some species in the genus *Diplodactylus (williamsi, ciliaris, elderi)* possess glands on the upper surface of the tail that produce a lymph-like sticky substance. This can be sprayed at predators to a distance of up to 50 cm.

The Madagascar flat-tailed geckos *(Uroplatus)* and the Southeast Asian geckos of the genus *Ptychozoon* have skin-folds on the sides of the tail, the flanks, the extremities, and the head that aid in camouflage. In *Ptychozoon* the well developed flap of skin along the flanks is not used for camouflage as it is folded under the body when the animal is at rest. The flap is used for semi-gliding or stability when the gecko jumps.

In addition to these special adaptations, geckos can shed their tails in time of danger (autotomy) like many other lizard species. The predator then becomes occupied with the tail while the gecko makes its escape. The missing tail is regenerated, but the replacement usually shows a simpler arrangement of scales and colors. Often these regenerated tails are shorter and do not possess the properties (adhesion, gripping, etc.) of the original. If a tail is damaged (i.e., only partly severed) it is not unusual to see a forked tail develop with two or more tips!

Many geckos show their mood by wagging the tail. When hunting for prey or during courtship activities, tail wagging signals the degree of excitement in the animal.

Underview of the rear end of *Ptychozoon* species, showing the large blunt cloacal bones or spurs and the pre-anal pores. Photo by Kenneth T. Nemuras.

The eyes of geckos are among the most beautiful objects in nature. Notice the delicate patterns of the *Uroplatus fimbriatus* above and the *Cyrtodactylus pulchellus* below. Photo above by R. G. Sprackland, that below by Kenneth T. Nemuras.

The Senses

The eye is the gecko's most important sense organ because the animal orients itself optically. In crepuscular and nocturnal species the eye is specially developed.

The light-sensitive area of the eye (the retina) contains many nerve cells and fibers, as well as a layer of optic cells. These optic cells consist of rods and cones, the former to aid sight in dark conditions, the latter to give sight in strong light and to aid color recognition. While the cones are considered to be the original optic cells, the rods (probably evolved from cones) constitute a phylogenetic development to aid night activity that is not confined only to geckos. The Wall Gecko *(Tarentola mauritanica)*, the Banded Desert Gecko *(Coleonyx variegatus)*, and other night-active geckos have developed a retina consisting only of rods that provides excellent sight in twilight conditions but does not allow color recognition. Whether other geckos, particularly diurnal species, can recognize colors has not been adequately researched.

The perception and recognition of the finest details seem to play a secondary role in the gecko's sight, as only a few species possess a fovea in the retinal structure. (The fovea is a depression in the retina containing only closely packed cone cells and is therefore a specialization for acute vision.)

Many crepuscular and

Stenodactylus petrii, a sand-dwelling gecko with fringed toes. Photo by R. D. Bartlett

nocturnal animals (for example: cats, crocodiles, pythons, vipers, geckos) possess vertical slit-like pupils. In geckos the elliptical pupil can be closed, leaving two, three, or four pinhole-sized openings. Until fairly recently it was thought that these little windows acted as intensifiers of

turned on.

Another theory considers the elliptical pupil to be a protective device for nocturnal geckos that sometimes bask in the sun; they must protect their rod-lined retina from strong sunlight. An elliptical pupil can be closed more completely than a circular

poor light, working like little shutters, the images from each one being superimposed on the retina and thus increasing the light intensity.

This theory can be discounted by any gecko keeper who approaches his terrarium at night and turns on the lights. He will see that the gecko's pupils are wide open in the dark and close only when the light is

The fully dilated pupil of *Phelsuma madagascariensis grandis* is readily visible here. Photo by Kenneth T. Nemuras.

The Painted Dwarf Gecko, *Lygodactylus picturatus*. Photo by H. Zimmermann.

function of eye-cleaning. It is true that many geckos lick over the brille with their tongue, but this is also done by the leopard gecko, which has movable eyelids! One can surmise that this habit arose before the evolution of the brille.

The gecko ear is more highly developed than that of most other lizard types. *Coleonyx variegatus* possesses an optimal hearing range of 300–1000 Hertz (Hz.), the same as that of a guinea pig. However, the guinea pig is able to perceive waves of 100,000 Hz., while the upper

one. An indication that this theory is plausible is that all day geckos of the genera *Phelsuma, Lygodactylus, Pristrurus,* and *Quendenfeldia,* as well as all of the Sphaerodactylinae, have circular pupils.

Only members of the subfamily Eublepharinae (eyelid geckos) possess movable eyelids. All other geckos have a transparent, immovable disc (known as the brille) covering the eye, similar to that found in snakes, the flap-footed lizards, the night lizards, and some skinks. The brille has evolved by a fusion of the upper and lower eyelids. The fact that such a brille has been developed by a wide selection of nocturnal reptiles shows that it is an efficient protective device.

It is commonly thought that, as movable eyelids are absent, the tongue has taken over the

Phelsuma cepediana, the Blue-tailed Day Gecko. Photo by Burkhard Kahl.

The eyelids are easily visible on this Reticulated or Big Bend Gecko, *Coleonyx reticulatus*. Photo by R. T. Zappalorti.

limit of hearing in lizards, including geckos, ends at 10,000 Hz. The higher development in the hearing of geckos compared to other lizards has a definite relationship with the ability of these reptiles to vocalize. In lizards the complicated structure of the ear is not concerned only with hearing; it is also an organ of balance.

In many gecko species calcium deposits are visible on the underside of the neck region as little sacs containing a milky solution of calcium carbonate. It can be considered that these constitute a reserve of calcium in gecko females for the production of hard-shelled eggs. There are some facts that support this theory: the sacs become more prominent during reproductive phases, and geckos that lay soft-shelled eggs (Eublepharinae and Diplodactylinae) do not possess these endolymphatic sacs.

Paradoxically however, the males also possess the calcium sacs, which may somewhat dampen the theory that the deposits are concerned just with the development of hard-shelled eggs. They are also found in many anoles, chameleons of the genus *Brookesia*, and the agamid *Cophotis ceylonica*. All these are climbing species so the sacs could be regarded as static (balance) organs.

A typical characteristic of many geckos is their ability to vocalize. The subfamily Eublepharinae and most species in the subfamilies

Right: A barking gecko, *Ptenopus garrulus*, sitting in its burrow in the Kalahari Desert. Photo by K. H. Switak.

Below: *Phelsuma standingi*, a day gecko. Notice the pendulent calcium sacs on the neck of this adult. Photo by Kenneth T. Nemuras.

Geckos have large, broad tongues that usually are notched. Photo of *Eublepharis macularius* by Kenneth T. Nemuras.

Diplodactylinae and Gekkoninae possess a voice, while members of the Sphaerodactylinae are voiceless. Gecko voices vary from quiet insect-like chirrups and squeaks to loud clucks and barks. Examples of the latter include the Tokay and the South African barking geckos of the genus *Ptenopus*. Little information is available on the function of the gecko voice, nor do we have sufficient data on whether the females of many species are capable of uttering sounds. In barking geckos, the evening chorus seems to be concerned with territorial factors, while the call of the Tokay attracts male and female to each other. In some species

the voice helps in partner selection. I have observed this several times in *Heteronotia binoei* and *Hemitheconyx caudicinctus*, in which male and female in the mating season have called to each other. The *Heteronotia* pair even performed a sort of answering game in which the female answered the male each time he called. A similar duet is performed by *Cyrtodactylus kotschyi* in Israel. In many geckos the voice is also used to shock predators, as most vocal geckos will squeak or hiss when captured. The loud call of the Tokay recently has been a factor in its popularity.

The sense of smell is also an important part of the gecko's life. Like most other reptiles, the sense of smell is closely connected with the function of the Jacobson's organ. A pair of these organs is situated in the palate, corresponding to the nostrils, and they are sensitive to scent particles. Although this organ is well developed in geckos, it seems to play only a minor part in odor perception. The gecko will test objects with its wide tongue, which is, however, poorly equipped to transfer scent particles to the Jacobson's organs. Geckos tend to use the nose more for the purpose of detecting odors. One can often observe the animals placing their noses near food items or sexual partners in order to smell them. Gravid females frequently smell a potential site before laying the eggs.

The gecko tongue is very motile and often is used to clean the eyes and face as in this *Phelsuma standingi*. Photo by Kenneth T. Nemuras.

REPRODUCTION, GROWTH, AND LONGEVITY

There are few detailed reports on the reproductive behavior of geckos, and the triggering mechanism for sexual activity in many species is unknown. Those species that live in temperate zones are brought into breeding condition by seasonal factors and the varying lengths of day and night. Therefore, the majority of such species mate in the spring, but sometimes a second pairing will take place in the fall. Given a short winter rest and an artificial day-length, captive specimens can be stimulated to mate. A stimulus can also be brought on by bringing the sexes together shortly before the breeding season.

In tropical regions there are some gecko species that are ready to breed at any time of the year and others that breed only at particular times. Geckos from subtropical and temperate regions of the Southern Hemisphere pair in our Northern Hemisphere fall or winter. Therefore, at least in the first year of their captivity, climatic conditions similar to those found in their habitat must be provided. Later one can endeavor to acclimate them to a reversal of the seasons.

The pairing behavior of geckos is closely tied to their nocturnal habits and often takes place under cover. Many species mate at the beginning of the normal main activity time.

In most gecko species, courtship and mating are similar to that of other types of lizards.

Right: A young and very delicate *Coleonyx variegatus*, the Banded Desert Gecko. Photo by Kenneth T. Nemuras.

Facing page: Underview of the cloacal region of a Tokay Gecko, *Gekko gecko*, showing the well developed pre-anal pored scales. Not very obvious cloacal bones or tubercles also can be seen in this male. Photo by Michael Gilroy.

Coleonyx reticulatus is nocturnal, difficult to collect, and poorly known. Photo by K. H. Switak.

After a long or short ritualized foreplay (standing sideways, waggling the tail, sniffing the female cloaca), the male approaches the female from the rear, climbs onto her, bites her in the neck, and brings his cloaca into apposition to hers. To copulate, only one of the two hemipenes is brought into action. The male Banded Desert Gecko *(Coleonyx variegatus)* possesses post-anal tubercles on the sides of the base of his tail that help him to hold the female cloaca open. As many geckos possess these tubercles and as they are more strongly developed in males, it can be surmised that other species also use them for this purpose.

For successful breeding results, it is essential to be able

to distinguish the sexes. A color difference (color dimorphism) is to be found only in a few species; for example, in the genera *Lygodactylus* and *Gonatodes* males have colorful head markings.

In many gecko species the male can be distinguished from the female by the thick tail-base, which is caused by the presence of the inverted hemipenes. In many cases males have larger and broader heads and are more sturdily built than females. Pre-anal, femoral, and post-anal tubercles may be present in both sexes, but they are more highly

A male Yellow-headed Gecko, *Gonatodes albo-gularis*, sexable by the head coloration. Photo by Kenneth T. Nemuras.

Male geckos (right) often show tubercles behind the cloacal opening and have a widened tail base to house the hemipenes.

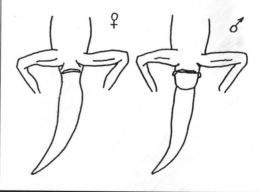

Hemidactylus garnotii, one of the several species of gecko known to be parthenogenetic, reproducing without males. Photo by S. McKeown.

Copulating *Phelsuma madagascariensis*, the cloacas being held in apposition so a hemipene can be inserted. Photo by Rolf Heselhaus.

developed in the male.

One method of distinguishing the sexes without handling the reptiles is to study the shed skin. The sloughed skin of the male has two globular shapes near the tail-base, the shed skin of the hemipenes.

In addition to these distinguishing marks, the behavior of the geckos, including territoriality and courtship, can give an idea of the sexes.

Three gecko species (*Hemidactylus garnotii*, *Lepidodactylus lugubris*, and *Gehyra ogasawarasimae*) are known to be parthenogenetic (capable of producing young without fertilization by the male). Only females typically are found in populations of these species; males are very rare or even absent. The females lay eggs from which only further females hatch. This method has many advantages as the reptiles colonize new territory, for one female and one egg can start a new population. Two of the species *(H. garnotii* and *L. lugubris)* have already populated an enormous area.

All geckos are oviparous (egg-laying) with the exception of the New Zealand genera *Heteropholis, Hoplodactylus,* and *Naultinus* and the New Caledonia species *Rhacodactylus trachyrhynchus,* which give birth to two live young.

Gecko eggs are soft-shelled or hard-shelled depending on the subfamily and have a globular or oval form. The size varies, depending on the species, from 3.5–32 mm. Incubation time in the wild is usually from two to three months. In captivity, incubation times of 35–183 days have been recorded. The soft-shelled eggs of the Eublepharinae and the Diplodactylinae require a humid medium in which to incubate (for details, see *Eublepharis macularius),* while the less sensitive hard-shelled eggs require a drier, warmer climate (28–32°C and 45–65% relative humidity). For the incubation of hard-shelled eggs, little transparent plastic boxes (10 x 10 x 5 cm) are ideal. The bottom of the box is covered with a layer of fine sand, filter paper, or foam rubber. Each week one or two drops of water are added to the substrate in order to maintain

A large juvenile Leopard Gecko, *Eublepharis macularius,* with the adult spotted pattern partially developed. Photo by Dr. Guido Dingerkus.

A pair of *Phelsuma* eggs laid in the axil of a plant. Photo by Kenneth T. Nemuras.

an adequate humidity. The eggs themselves should not be made damp or wet.

Parental protection is, to date, scarcely known among the geckos, although a few species protect their eggs for a few hours after oviposition. Females of *Eublepharis macularius*, *Hemitheconyx caudicinctus*, and *Pachydactylus tigrinus* will jump at a predator and attempt to bite. The male Tokay guards the eggs and the small young.

Many gecko species have communal egg-laying areas, including all European species, *Gekko g. gecko*, *Lepidodactylus lugubris*, and *Ptyodactylus hasselquistii*.

Young geckos grow very quickly—many species are sexually mature at the beginning of their second year and almost full-sized. With optimum terrarium conditions and adequate feeding, young geckos can develop so quickly that they are sexually mature in the first year. *Paroedura pictus* from Madagascar is such an example. There are, however, other extremes. Even with good feeding, the Wall Gecko (*Tarentola mauritanica*) requires four or five years to reach maturity; in the wild it would probably take longer. A forced development can shorten the lives of our terrarium animals.

Longevity in geckos has been studied many times in the past, but exact ages of only a few species have been documented. In most cases these have applied to captive animals.

Above: Newly emerged hatchling of *Phelsuma* species. Photo by R. G. Sprackland. Below: An adult and hatchling of *Pachydactylus* species from Namibia. Such differences in coloration are not common in geckos. Photo by Paul Freed.

Naultinus elegans, a New Zealand Green Gecko. These are among the few live-bearing geckos, perhaps an adaptation to the often harsh climatic conditions of New Zealand. Photo by K. H. Switak.

KEEPING GECKOS

Foods and Feeding

In the wild, geckos feed on a variety of insects and spiders, even small vertebrates. Some species supplement their diet with fruits (banana, mango, etc.) or they lap up fruit juice or nectar from flowers. The Tokay has been observed devouring small snakes and nestling birds. Some geckos eat other species of geckos; others practice cannibalism on young examples of their own species.

The most valuable food for terrarium geckos is still "meadow plankton" (a variety of small insects, spiders, etc., captured by passing a fine-meshed insect sweeping net through long grass and other herbage). One must, however, ensure that such food is free of insecticides, herbicides, and other such pollution. As some terrarium keepers are suspicious of meadow plankton for this reason, they tend not to use it. Many compromise foods have been used with success.

The most important food insect is the cricket. The best type seems to be the two-spotted cricket, *Gryllus bimaculatus*. Other species are also suitable. *Acheta domesticus* is taken greedily by geckos and is ideal as an easily digested tonic for geckos suffering transport stress. As the staple diet, you

Small plastic enclosures are ideal for geckos that 1) need to be quarantined; 2) are very small; and 3) are going to travel. Such enclosures are quite inexpensive and can be found at most pet shops. Photo courtesy of Hagen.

should use *G. bimaculatus*, however, as *A. domesticus* is low in roughage.

Another important food insect is the wax moth (*Galleria melonella*), of which mainly the larvae but also the adults are used. The adult moths are eaten by many geckos, but, in spite of this, you should not use them as the main food, only as a change or as a supplement. Wax moth larvae are very fattening (ca. 19% fat) and should therefore be given sparingly. Like *A. domesticus*, the larva of the wax moth is easily digested and is ideal as a tonic for weak individuals. Should a shortage of crickets occur, it is better to bridge the gap with wax moth larvae than with mealworms or the smaller grain beetles and their larvae.

Small species of geckos and young geckos can be fed with fruitflies (*Drosophila*). Fruitflies alone, however, will not allow your young geckos to develop satisfactorily and become sexually mature. Many species of flies may be used as a substitute food; some *Hemidactylus* species will eat flies greedily.

Many steppe and desert geckos feed on various beetles that would be impossible to supply in the terrarium. A substitute insect for such geckos is the Argentine cockroach (*Blaptica dubia*). Fully grown, these insects cannot be used as they reach 40 mm in length. The developing nymphs from 5 mm upward, however, will be taken

eagerly by many ground-dwelling species.

The procurement of food insects is today no longer a problem. There are many specialist dealers who get supplies of crickets, wax moths, etc., on a regular basis. Anyone who keeps more than a pair of geckos, however, should make the effort to breed some food insects. This allows you to improve the nutritional quality of the insects by feeding them well and prevents the problems associated with waiting for commercial deliveries. A colony of crickets and of wax moths should be adequate, but, depending on the types of geckos being kept, fruitflies or houseflies may also be bred. A breeding colony of Argentine cockroaches may also be useful. If you keep large gecko species (*Eublepharis, Hemitheconyx, Gekko, Thecadactylus*), a small breeding colony of mice will prove useful.

An important factor in gecko nutrition is an adequate supply of calcium and phosphorus. Many nutritional problems (soft-jaw in *Phelsuma* species and in juveniles of other species) and reproductive problems arise from a deficiency of these elements. For healthy development of the bones, mammals require a calcium-phosphorus ratio of 1.2:1. The insects that we mainly use to feed our geckos mostly contain an excess of phosphorus. Assuming geckos require a similar calcium-phosphorus ratio as mammals,

Large Leopard Geckos, *Eublepharis macularius*, will take large food items, including baby pink mice. They also will take other lizards, so be careful. Photo by Burkhard Kahl.

it is obvious that a supplementary supply of calcium must be given. In addition, supplementary vitamins are important, particularly vitamin D_3, which is barely present in the insect food.

Calcium can be given by sprinkling a powdered supplement over the slightly dampened food insects before giving them to the animals. Vitamins can be mixed into the water spray or drinking water. Good supplements should be water-soluble (2–3 drops in 1.5 liters of water). Vitamin D_3 and multivitamin products should not be given without giving calcium at the same time, otherwise demineralization of the bones may result.

Gecko Terraria and Their Accessories

All-glass terraria are ideal for keeping and breeding geckos. Should you wish to avoid the regular cleaning of the glass, however, you can use opaque synthetic material for the floor, sides, and back. Both materials are similar in price and weight. Simple diagonal ventilation, from the bottom of the front to the top of the back, is adequate in most cases. Problems with the access doors can occur with gecko terraria. As we are dealing with small, agile creatures, sliding doors, particularly double ones, are not always the answer. Even sticking foam rubber in the gap between the slides is not always

Fortunately, there now are thermometers designed to monitor the high gradients that are natural to reptile-keeping. **Below:** Undertank heating pads are ideal for geckos. Warmth can be provided in only one particular section of the enclosure, leaving the remaining area cooler, thus giving the animal(s) freedom of choice. Photos courtesy of Hagen.

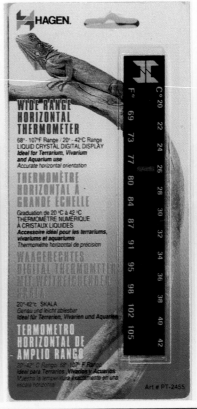

Beddings that are light and easy to work with, such as the bark bedding shown here, are ideal for gecko keepers. Such beddings can be found at most pet shops and purchased in bulk quantities. Photo courtesy of Four Paws.

the best solution. Most gecko terraria should have a single sliding door or, if several cases are standing in a row, a hinged door.

For nocturnal geckos, lighting with Osram-Lumilux or Philips-TLD Super 80 fluorescent tubes (daylight type) and equivalents should be adequate. One or two tubes can be used, depending on the dimensions of the cage. Diurnal geckos such as *Phelsuma, Lygodactylus, Gonatodes,* and *Pristrurus* require lighting that also provides ultraviolet rays, such as Truelite™ fluorescent tubes. There are other types that emit ultraviolet rays, but you should be sure that they are UV-A rays and not the hard UV-C rays.

Check with your pet dealer to find suitable equivalent bulbs. Plant bulbs are usually not suitable.

You can use the fluorescent tube starter for heating the floor and the air space. The equipment must be earthed and built-in in such a way that the animals cannot burn themselves. Dampness should not be allowed to enter the equipment. Additional heating for the air space can be provided with simple tungsten incandescent bulbs, which are available in various wattages. A silicone-covered heat cable (expensive, but it does not become hard and brittle so quickly) or a heating pad may also be used to heat the substrate. Any of the heaters

Geckos from more moderate habitats will need plants and climbing branches, as well as a small water bowl for humidity. Many geckos get their water by licking dew and raindrops from leaves and rocks, so the terrarium should be sprayed regularly with room-temperature water. Adequate ventilation is necessary to prevent the growth of fungus and stagnation of the air.

mentioned should preferably be controlled with a thermostat so the danger of over-heating is minimized. A further sophistication is the installation of a timer to control switching on and off.

Tiny juvenile geckos can be reared in plastic boxes or small glass aquaria. The lids of such containers should consist of gauze, and there may be gauze panels in the sides. Be sure that these small containers are adequately ventilated and do not overheat.

Diseases and Parasites

Very little information is available on the diseases and parasites of geckos. This may be due to the fact that it is very difficult to diagnose diseases in

these little lizards. In addition, dead geckos are not frequently sent for pathological examination. However, geckos that are kept in optimal conditions are unlikely to suffer from any major problems. Most deaths occur not so much from diseases or parasites as from inadequate husbandry, a deficiency of minerals, or an imbalanced calcium-phosphorus ratio.

External parasites, mainly mites, have been observed on some gecko species in the wild, but they are rarely found in the terrarium. The same goes for ticks. The tiny, deep red mites are usually found in groups along the flanks, around the ears, and between the toes. They do not seem to greatly affect the host animal (in contrast to snake mites, which can cause anemia). Gecko mites do not reproduce as quickly as snake mites. By applying liver–oil salve to the groups of mites for several days, they will be slowly destroyed. Take care that the salve does not come into contact with the adhesive foot pads of geckos that have them. Little information is available regarding the control of ectoparasites with chemical treatments. Spraying or bathing the infected animals with Neguvon has been recommended. Lung mites are rarely found in geckos, but should they occur they can cause damage. Treatment of this ailment is to date unknown.

Internal parasites such as nematodes (threadworms) and cestodes (tapeworms) are also found in geckos, but in normal situations they are not dangerous. The infection of further animals with tapeworms is not likely, as these worms require an intermediate host unlikely to be found in the terrarium. Threadworms also find it difficult to reproduce in a hygienically kept terrarium (usually with a warm, dry substrate). The fact that many geckos have particular defecation sites makes cleaning easy. Control of threadworms can (with veterinary assistance) be carried out with Panacur at 30–50 mg per kilogram of body weight.

Bacterial infections are fairly

Gehyra mutilata, a gecko that has proven very adaptable, adjusting to the climates on numerous Pacific islands to which it has been accidentally introduced. Photo by S. McKeown.

Foot of *Gekko gecko*, the Tokay. Mites occasionally are found at the bases of the toes, but they seldom are a serious threat to health. Photo by Kenneth T. Nemuras.

common in lizards and are known to occur in geckos. One can avoid such diseases by keeping the animals in optimum conditions so they maintain their natural resistance.

One of the gecko keeper's most feared ailments is the so-called "shiver and cramp" disease. The afflicted animal usually stands in the terrarium and its whole body shakes. Such an infected animal will usually die within a few days. Even an oral dose of multivitamin preparation (3 drops in 250 ml water) will not save a sick animal. It is suspected that the disease is caused by a deficiency of calcium or phosphorus or an incorrect ratio of these minerals.

Mouth rot in *Phelsuma* species, jaw tumors in *Cyrtodactylus caspius*, and fatty liver in juveniles (*Eublepharis macularius, Paroedura pictus*) may all be caused by inadequate husbandry. As so little is known about gecko diseases, it is the responsibilty of the keeper to do everything in his power to give his animals the best captive conditions. Should a disease still occur, you can only try the medicines and treatments successful with other lizards and hope for the best. Results will depend on whether you can get the dosages right for these little lizards.

EYELID GECKOS
(SUBFAMILY EUBLEPHARINAE)

The Eublepharinae is the oldest subfamily of the modern geckos. There are two genera each in Asia, Africa, and America. The Asian members are *Aeluroscalabotes* (two species) and *Eublepharis* (six species, including the well-known and popular terrarium animal *E. macularius*, the Leopard Gecko). In Africa we have *Hemitheconyx* and *Holodactylus*, each with two species. *Anarbylus* (one species, usually considered part of *Coleonyx*, thus making *Anarbylus* a synonym of *Coleonyx*) and *Coleonyx* (five species) are the American representative of this gecko subfamily.

The main characteristic of the members of this subfamily is the movable eyelids, which are not possessed by any other subfamily; they are not replaced by brilles.

Another characteristic of this subfamily is the presence of claws on the toes and the absence of adhesive lamellae on the feet. Unlike other geckos, members of this subfamily reproduce with two soft-shelled eggs. These are more difficult to hatch than the eggs of other geckos; during the incubation period they can stand only a very minimal range of substrate and air humidity.

The recently increased

Eublepharis macularius, the Leopard Gecko, is perhaps the most popular gecko and certainly the most common eyelid gecko. Photo by Kenneth T. Nemuras.

availability of Leopard Geckos has made this subfamily perhaps the most important among pet geckos.

Eublepharis macularius Leopard Gecko

RANGE: Eastern Iran, SE Afghanistan, Pakistan, NW India.

HABITAT: Found in steppe areas and in mountains to 2100 m. Hides in burrows or under rocks during the day. At dusk it emerges and moves high-legged in search of its prey.

DESCRIPTION: With a length of 250 mm, this species is one of the largest geckos. It has movable eyelids. The outer ear is prominent. The toes are equipped with a diagonal row of lamellae that, however, are not adhesive. There are strong claws on the ends of the toes. The tail is round and ringed.

The ground color is light to dark yellow with numerous irregular spots and blotches. No two animals possess the same spot pattern. Those from Pakistan are more heavily

Leopard Geckos are at home in the dry, rocky plains of south-central Asia, a factor that has made them more adaptable to the terrarium. Photo by H. Hansen.

In the adult Leopard Gecko the blotches of the young are replaced with small rounded spots. Notice the simple toes without lamellae. Photo by Michael Gilroy.

spotted than those from Afghanistan. There are some individuals that retain part of the juvenile banded pattern. Some examples from the area of New Delhi (N India) even lean toward longitudinal banding.

The belly is plain white. The body is covered with tiny scales, but there are large tubercles on the rear of the head, the back, the tail, and the extremities. On the flanks, these tubercles are often crowded together in greater numbers.

BIOLOGY, CARE, AND BREEDING: A breeding group consisting of a male and three or four females requires a terrarium 100 x 40 x 40 cm. Each animal must have its own hiding place. Coarse sand or a mixture of sand and earth can be used as a substrate. A part of the substrate can be made from a mixture of sand and potting compost; this should be kept damp and have a temperature of about 30°C. This will be used by the females as an egg-laying site. Plants are not strictly necessary, but a shallow water dish is essential so that the geckos can slake their thirst.

Leopard Geckos are often seen using the tongue to wipe the face and eyes. The exact function of this behavior is uncertain, although it almost certainly has to do with removing particles of sand, etc., from the face. Photo by Kenneth T. Nemuras.

Adult Leopard Geckos have strong jaws capable of crushing a large grasshopper...and giving the keeper a good pinch on the fingers. Photo by Michael Gilroy.

The geckos will be happy with a daytime temperature of 28–32°C, cooled at night to 20–22°C. A small part of the substrate should be heated to 35°C.

It is recommended that these geckos be given a simulated hibernation period of two to four weeks at lower temperatures (daytime 18–22°C, nightime around 15°C). Starting in September, gradually decrease the daily length of lighting from 12–14 hours to 6–8 hours. In January gradually increase it again.

In these circumstances the geckos will mate at the end of January or beginning of February. The first eggs will be laid at the beginning of March. The females can produce two or perhaps three clutches per year. The two soft-shelled eggs (27–32 x 15–16 mm) are buried in a suitable spot in the substrate.

If the eggs are laid in a spot specially prepared for them, they can stay there for incubation. You must, however, ensure that the air humidity remains constant and the daytime temperature is maintained at

An adult Leopard Gecko, *Eublepharis macularius*. Photo by Ken Lucas, Steinhart Aquarium.

Heads of juvenile (above) and adult (below) Leopard Geckos. Photo above by W. Mudrack, that below by Kenneth T. Nemuras.

A banded juvenile (above) and a spotted adult (below) Leopard Gecko. Photo above by W. Mudrack, that below by H. Hansen.

It is not uncommon for juvenile geckos to differ somewhat from their parents, but they normally are easily recognizable. In juveniles the contrasts of colors often are stronger, the colors purer and brighter. Bands tend to break up with age, and saddles or blotches often split. Middorsal lines may disappear with age. Structurally a juvenile resembles the adult in most details, including lamellae under the toes and presence or absence of tubercles, although both may increase somewhat with growth. Leopard Geckos present one of the most confusing color changes among common geckos, accentuated by the change in bulk from the delicate juvenile to the robust adult. Photo of adult Leopard Gecko above by Burkhard Kahl, that of juvenile at right by Michael Gilroy.

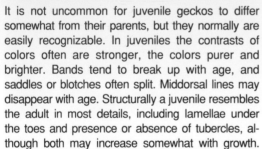

around 30°C (cooling at night will do no harm). An inverted flowerpot placed over the laying site will protect the eggs and the newly hatched young from the voracious adults that would not think twice before eating them.

In most cases, this method works without the loss of youngsters, not only with Leopard Geckos but also with other species.

The eggs may also be incubated in an incubator. A small aquarium with a capacity of 20–30 liters is filled with 3–4 cm of water and heated with an aquarium heater and thermostat so the air temperature is maintained at 29–30°C. A brick is placed in the water, and the incubation box (a plastic sandwich box) is placed on top of it. Incubation medium

consists of a mixture of sand and potting compost. A gauze lid or piece of pantyhose is stretched over the container to prevent the young geckos from falling into the water when they hatch. The aquarium is covered with a sheet of glass so a high humidity will build up. The incubation medium must not become wet from condensed water. Prevent this by laying a small sheet of glass over the incubation box. A matchstick under each corner will ensure that air exchange between the incubation box and the aquarium can take place.

The most important factor in hatching soft-shelled eggs is that a constant humidity is maintained in the air and in the hatching medium. The eggs can be damaged by excessive damp

Because Leopard Geckos currently are being bred in large numbers, they have become very common in the pet market, especially as large juveniles. Photo by Dr. Guido Dingerkus.

An adult *Hemitheconyx caudicinctus*, the African Clawed Gecko or Fat-tailed Gecko. Photo by Ken Lucas, Steinhart Aquarium.

and by arid conditions, but slight variations in temperature seem to do no harm.

Depending on the conditions, the young will hatch in 39–62 days. They are 83–90 mm long, weigh about 3.6 grams, and are marked differently from the adults. Young Leopard Geckos have three black bands across the back and four on the tail, but these soon develop into the adult spotted pattern. The young are eager to feed, and rearing rarely presents any particular problems. They are usually sexually mature and almost fully grown at 18 months.

As with many other gecko species, you can run only a single Leopard Gecko male with a number of females as they are extremely aggressive. Males differ from females in that they are more robustly built, have a larger and wider head, and have an angular row of 9–14 pre-anal pores.

The beautiful color and pattern and the ease with which they may be kept and bred make Leopard Geckos highly recommended for the beginner.

RELATED SPECIES: *Eublepharis kuroiwae,* with three subspecies (*kuroiwae, orientalis, splendens*), lives on the Ryukyus of southern Japan. Depending on the subspecies, they reach a head and body length of 80–90 cm, the total length being around 160 mm. *E. kuroiwae* is a slender species with a pointed head and attractive coloration. The dark brown back is crossed by four pink bands, and the pink color also extends onto the upper sides of the limbs. The tail is black with white bands, some of which are incomplete. The males do not possess pre-anal or femoral pores, but their well developed hemipenal sacs render them easily distinguishable from the females.

To match its habitat, this

species requires a warm, humid terrarium with plants and dry hiding places. Daytime temperature should be maintained around 28°C. In such a terrarium, this beautiful nocturnal gecko should do well on a diet of crickets, grasshoppers, etc. No information is available regarding its reproduction. A female laid two soft-shelled eggs (15–17 x 9–10 mm) twice in 29 days in my terrarium, but these failed to hatch.

Due to its rarity and relatively difficult husbandry, *Eublepharis kuroiwae* should be kept only by experienced persons.

Hemitheconyx caudicinctus African Clawed Gecko

Range: West Africa from Senegal to northern Cameroon.

Habitat: Open, dry woodland, savannah, and rocky hillsides. The climate in these areas is affected by rainy and dry seasons.

Description: The general build

An exquisitely patterned juvenile African Clawed Gecko. Photo by R. D. Bartlett.

of this species is not unlike that of the Leopard Gecko, but the tip of the snout, the toes, and the tail are somewhat different. The snout is more rounded, the toes shorter and with weaker claws. The tail is slightly whorled and plump, the latter more prominent in regenerated tails that have a blunt rather than a pointed tip.

The color pattern consists of light and dark brown transverse bands that are separated by rows of white spots that can sometimes merge into narrow bands. A seldom-found variety possesses a wide white stripe extending from the top of the head to the tail. This form is not, as was previously thought, the result of sexual dimorphism, as it may be seen in either sex.

BIOLOGY, CARE, AND BREEDING: Little is yet known about the biology of this species. It is believed to estivate in the dry season as it is rarely found during this period. The fat reserves in the tail undoubtedly help the animal during this time.

With the exception of a few very aggressive examples, this species can be considered relatively docile. It moves through the terrarium with a slow, deliberate gait. Faster movements may be seen when food is introduced. It is not a particularly good climber, due to its poorly developed claws. Apart from small juveniles that will sit in diagonal branches, this species stays mainly on the terrarium floor.

Although it is definitely a nocturnally active species in the wild, it will become used to feeding during the day in the terrarium. This species will rarely become as tame and trusting, accepting food from the hand, as the Leopard Gecko.

With a length of 210 mm, this species can be kept in a group of one male and two females in a terrarium with a minimum size of 60 x 40 x 40 cm. The substrate may consist of a mixture of sand and potting compost or a mixture of river sand and loam. Although planting is not strictly necessary because the geckos rarely climb, the back wall of the terrarium can be decorated with plants. Shallow plant pots filled with a mixture of sand and potting compost may be used as egg-laying sites by the females. Tubes of cork bark or earthenware can be set in the substrate to act as hiding places for the geckos. A shallow vessel containing clean drinking water plus a vitamin supplement should always be available.

The substrate may be heated with a cable to 30–35°C. The hiding places should vary in temperature so that the animals can seek out cooler spots if they wish. The air temperature may reach 32°C during the day but should be reduced to about 20°C at night. Temperatures as low as 17°C will do no harm. The terrarium interior should be lightly sprayed every other day. Feeding is as described for *E. macularius*.

The distinctive striped variant of *Hemitheconyx caudicinctus*. Photo by Kenneth T. Nemuras.

Hemitheconyx caudicinctus has rarely been bred in captivity. The difficulty seems to be the provision of the correct climatic conditions (wet and dry seasons and the estivation) in the terrarium. A further factor is the difficulty in incubating soft-shelled eggs. In the wild, it seems that pairing takes place in October/November and the eggs are laid in January/February. The youngsters probably hatch halfway through the dry season, in April.

In the terrarium, an increasing readiness to mate can be observed about the end of November to the end of December. Initially, the defensive actions of the females are very strong, and the animals face each other sideways and threaten each other. A few days later the male becomes more persistent and endeavors to mount the female. The male bites the female on the neck quite fiercely, in a manner normally used only on rival males. In addition, he tries to push his tail under that of the female. If the female is not yet ready to accept him, she will constantly try to escape and pairing will fail. The male will then change to "softer" tactics by biting the female gently along the flanks in order to stimulate her, but it may take several days before he is successful. During copulation, the male holds his partner tightly by the neck. The female will hold her tail up so the cloacal openings can come into apposition.

A female normally lays two eggs that are buried in the substrate. Incubation times in the terrarium have varied from 60–77 days. The young geckos average 70 mm in length and are patterned differently from the adults. The ground color is greenish yellow with sharply defined brown patches. These are horse-shoe shaped and vary from dark olive-brown to grayish brown. Two broad transverse bands occur on the back, and the tail carries three dark violet-brown rings separated by light gray.

The male is distinguished from the female by a broader head, a more robust body, and brighter coloring. In addition, the male possesses 10–13 pre-anal pores.

Incubation of the eggs is as described for the Leopard Gecko. The eggs of *H. caudicinctus* seem to be less sensitive to the substrate temporarily drying out than those of the Leopard Gecko. The African Clawed Gecko is suitable for beginners.

Coleonyx variegatus
Banded Desert Gecko, Western Banded Gecko

RANGE: Southwestern USA (Utah, Nevada, Arizona, New Mexico, California, and Texas) and northern Mexico (Sonora, Sinaloa, Baja California, and the islands of Cedros, Santa Inez, and San Marcos).

HABITAT: Inhabits hilly desert areas.

DESCRIPTION: This American representative of the eyelid geckos is more slimly built than,

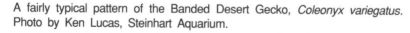

A fairly typical pattern of the Banded Desert Gecko, *Coleonyx variegatus*. Photo by Ken Lucas, Steinhart Aquarium.

Coleonyx switaki. Discovered in Baja California only a few years ago and described from a unique specimen, this distinctive gecko is now known to range north into California. Highly prized by collectors, it is poorly known and not often found. At first placed in a genus of its own, *Anarbylus*, Switak's Bare-toed Gecko is now considered to be a member of *Coleonyx*. Photo by K. H. Switak.

Two patterns of the Banded Desert Gecko, *Coleonyx variegatus*. Photo above by Alex Kerstitch, that below by Burkhard Kahl.

Coleonyx brevis, the Texas Desert Gecko, was long considered a subspecies of the Banded Desert Gecko. Photo by K. H. Switak.

for example, the Leopard Gecko. It does not grow as large, and an example with a length of 140 mm can be considered fully grown.

The ground color of the finely granular skin varies from yellow to light brown. Wide transverse brown bands that are lighter in the center extend along the back and tail.

BIOLOGY, CARE, AND BREEDING: In its natural range *C. variegatus* is active from April to October, although some adults may be found in March or November. The temperature range in which the species is active is 16–34°C. The optimum temperature is 28°C. During the main heat of the day it hides under stones or in burrows, coming out at night.

The breeding season begins in April and continues until July. The pairing behavior is only mildly ritualized. With his tail wagging and head held low, the male approaches the female from behind. He will then either throw himself at the female from a short distance or gently lick and then bite her tail. Biting of the back or the rear limbs has also been observed. The male then moves along the female's body until he is able to bite her neck, after which copulation begins.

Between May and September the female lays three or more clutches of two eggs. The soft-shelled eggs (0.85 gram) are buried in damp substrate material. In the terrarium, the eggs should be removed to an incubator and treated as described for *E. macularius*. At an incubation temperature of 22–30°C, the 57-mm-long juveniles will hatch out in 42–58 days. Incubation times of up to 81 days have also been reported.

The juveniles carry a relatively richer contrast of transverse bands than the adults, but they gradually assume adult coloration during growth. Young are simple to rear on small crickets and wax moth larvae and can be sexually mature in 10 months.

The sexes can be distinguished by examining the underside of the tail. The male possesses a pair of spurs about 1 mm in length; in the female these are absent or very poorly developed.

This species does not require very spacious housing, and a medium sized terrarium (60 x 40 x 40 cm) will be adequate for a male and three or four females. The substrate can consist of a sand and loam mixture, with a number of flat stones providing decoration and hiding places. Planting is optional, but a drinking vessel is essential. Feeding consists of the usual insects. Lighting, heating, and winter rest are as described for the Leopard Gecko.

RELATED SPECIES: The Texas Banded Gecko, *Coleonyx brevis*, occasionally appears on the market.

The Big Bend or Reticulated Gecko, *Coleonyx reticulatus*, was for many years known from only a single specimen, and it still is poorly known. Photo by R. D. Bartlett.

DOUBLE-FINGERED GECKOS
(SUBFAMILY DIPLODACTYLINAE)

Members of this subfamily are found only in Australia, New Zealand, New Caledonia, and the Loyalty Islands. The largest living gecko, *Rhacodactylus leachianus* (New Caledonia), is a member of this subfamily. (*Hoplodactylus delacourti* is larger but probably extinct.) Another interesting aspect of the subfamily is that the New Zealand genera *Heteropholis*, *Hoplodactylus*, *Naultinus*, and a New Caledonian giant gecko (*R. trachyrhynchus*) give birth to two live young rather than laying eggs. Other members of the subfamily normally lay two soft-shelled eggs.

The double-fingered geckos are capable of vocalizing. They have a brille over the eye. Calcium deposits are not present in the neck region. Adhesive toe-pads are not possessed by all members of the group.

Diplodactylus ciliaris
Spiny-tailed Gecko

RANGE: Australia (West Australia with the exception of the wide area in the south and southwest, Northern Territory, north and central South Australia, western Queensland, and a small area of northwestern New South Wales).

HABITAT: Very variable, ranging from tropical to desert regions.

DESCRIPTION: Very variable in color. The ground color ranges from silver-gray to dark brown,

The Striped Spiny-Tailed Gecko, *Diplodactylus vittatus*. Photo by Dr. Sherman Minton.

Notice the conspicuous tubercles on the tail of this *Diplodactylus conspicillatus* from Queensland, Australia. Photo by K. H. Switak.

with a few or numerous black, gray, white, and orange scales that sometimes are grouped to form bands. The unregenerated tail is covered with long spine-like scales that usually are colored orange or orange and black. Almost plain brown or gray specimens are known.

The irregular scales on the dorsal surface are globular and keeled, giving the skin a rough texture. Small spine-like scales may be included, sometimes grouped to form two or three longitudinal rows. A row of longer spine-like scales runs along the top of the tail. Spiny scales are also positioned above the eye.

The body is slender and the limbs relatively long. The tail is round or slightly flattened. The toes are narrow but carry a pair of large adhesive pads on their tips.

This colorful and bizarre species reaches a length of 140 mm (head and body 83 mm, tail 55 mm).

BIOLOGY, CARE, AND BREEDING: Mainly arboreal, but in desert regions it may become terrestrial. A single pair will do well and may breed in a small, dry terrarium (30 x 30 x 40 cm). The substrate may consist of sand. Two or three cork bark tubes and a plant pot (with or without plant) as an egg-laying site will be adequate furnishings. This species lays soft-shelled eggs, so a container of damp potting compost or peat/sand mixture is necessary. The geckos will obtain their drinking water from regular spraying. The daytime temperature can reach 28°C, reduced at night to 20–22°C.

The Spiny-tailed Gecko is a placid terrarium inhabitant. It may be fed upon the usual insect food. Under optimal terrarium conditions, the females can be very productive; in exceptional cases as many as six to eight clutches have been

produced in a single year. The soft-shelled oval eggs should be buried in a peat/sand mixture kept at a constant dampness (but not wet!). Incubated at a temperature of 26–29°C and 70–80% relative air humidity, the young will hatch in about 65 days. The juveniles are relatively easy to rear.

Sex determination is simple with this species. The males are more intensely colored and the root of the tail is much broader due to the hemipenes. The males also possess pre-anal tubercles.

This is a beautiful species that is simple to keep and breed, but

An adult velvet gecko, *Oedura castelnaui*, in which the pattern has begun to break up. Photo by K. H. Switak.

The Mottled Velvet Gecko, *Oedura marmorata*. The fine scales of velvet geckos are distinctive. Photo by R. G. Sprackland.

as only a few breeding groups are kept at present they are of limited availablity to beginners.

Oedura monilis
Ocellated Velvet Gecko

RANGE: Western slopes and mountain ranges in central and northern New South Wales and southeastern Queensland, Australia.

HABITAT: This species lives in woodland regions and is found mainly under the loose bark of dead trees.

DESCRIPTION: The dorsal surface is light yellow-brown with numerous reddish or bluish brown scales that form a marbled pattern. Five or six pairs of brown and white, cream, or bluish white "eye spots" (ocelli) are positioned on the back between the neck and the base of the tail. These eye spots can also be merged, forming a figure-8 shape or bands. The belly is whitish.

The scales of the upper body are round and not keeled, giving the skin a smooth appearance.

Oedura monilis reaches a total length of 150 mm. The head and body are 80 mm in length, the rest being taken up by the relatively slender and slightly flattened tail.

BIOLOGY, CARE, AND BREEDING: *O. monilis* requires terrarium conditions (furnishings, temperatures) similar to those for the Spiny-tailed Gecko. It is a placid species that goes hunting for food only after the terrarium light has been switched off. Feeding poses no problems; as well as the usual insect food, it will take earthworms and is not unknown to take little strips of pork! As it will attack other lizards, it should only be kept with geckos of a similar size. For

breeding, it is recommended that they be kept in individual pairs.

The breeding of this species is not particularly difficult. Females can be quite productive, producing five or more clutches per year in the terrarium. Such a productivity will only occur, however, when optimal conditions are maintained and a rich variety of food is available.

The soft-shelled eggs (20–24 x 10–13 mm) are buried by the female in a soft, slightly damp substrate. The eggs should be removed from the terrarium and placed in an incubator, as described for the Leopard Gecko. With an incubation temperature of 26–29°C and a 70–80% relative humidity, the young (head and body 33–38, tail 23–28 mm) will hatch in 50–60 days. The juveniles are beautifully colored and patterned, the violet-black ground color being marked from head to tail with two rows of black-bordered round to oval yellow spots. Rearing problems are minimal.

The young can be sexually mature at one year of age. Sex determination is simple: the root of the tail is much thicker in the male due to the inverted hemipenes.

The Ocellated Velvet Gecko is recommended for the more experienced herpetologist.

In the juvenile *Oedura castelnaui* the bands are solid, with few or no light scales within the dark areas. Completely banded patterns are common in juvenile geckos. Photo by K. H. Switak.

TYPICAL GECKOS
(SUBFAMILY GEKKONINAE)

The subfamily Gekkoninae contains the majority of living gecko species and is also the most widely distributed. In the Old World they occur between latitudes 40° South and 50° North, while in the New World they are found between 48° South and 35° North.

Typical geckos can vocalize, the eye is protected with a brille, adhesive lamellae on the toes may be present or absent, and so may pre-anal tubercles. Endolymph sacs are present in the neck region. Most species lay a clutch of two eggs, a few just one. At first the eggs are soft, but they soon harden. These calcium-shelled eggs often adhere to each other and are well protected against external conditions. Most gecko species kept in the terrarium are from this subfamily.

Alsophylax laevis
Southern Straight-fingered Gecko

RANGE: Southern USSR (Turkmenistan, Uzbekistan) and Afghanistan.

HABITAT: This species may be found near human habitations as often as it is found away from them. In Kabul (at 1800 m altitude), the capital city of Afghanistan, it is the most common gecko species. The earth houses with their numerous wall cavities provide it with a good habitat. In the USSR it is found on the stems of plants in desert areas.

DESCRIPTION: This is a small, slender species with an extremely flattened body. In contrast to the closely related Caspian Straight-fingered Gecko (*A. pipiens*), which has granulate and tubercular scales on its body, *A. laevis* has a homogenous scalation without large tubercular scales. The toes are straight and not widened; on the underside there is a row of smooth lamellae.

The Southern Straight-fingered Gecko can reach a total length of 90 mm, of which half is taken up by the tail.

The ground color varies from yellow through yellowish brown to gray-brown. The back is decorated with seven irregular dark brown transverse bands. On the tail there are 12 bands. Patternless specimens sometimes occur.

BIOLOGY, CARE, AND BREEDING: A small terrarium with a length of 30 cm is suitable for this species. Sand and fine gravel can be used as the substrate materials; cork bark and flat stones will provide hiding places. Depending on the area and the season, the lighting and heating are provided with a 40 or 60 watt tungsten bulb. This species does not require too high a temperature; 24–26°C is adequate, but the temperature under the bulb can reach 30°C.

Male (below) and female (above) barking geckos, *Ptenopus kochi*, from Namibia. These burrowing geckos are notorious for their dog-like voices. Photos by Paul Freed.

It is recommended that the geckos be allowed a four to six weeks winter "rest period" at 8–10°C, especially if breeding is contemplated. Also, the daily quota of light should be regulated to provide conditions as natural as possible (see *E. macularius*). The diet should be no problem, but it is important to lightly spray daily so the geckos can drink and a humidity level of 50% is maintained in the terrarium. This humidity level is important for trouble-free shedding.

The reproductive behavior of this species is poorly known. The pairing time is probably shortly after the end of the hibernation period. In the terrarium the females lay eggs between February and October. One or two hard-shelled eggs (5 x 4 mm, 0.320–0.325 g) per clutch may be buried or simply laid on the surface of the substrate. With a variable incubation temperature (daytime 28°C, nighttime 20°C) and normal air humidity (50–60%), the young will hatch in 44–93 days, averaging 52–58 days. The newly hatched juveniles, apart from a yellow tail, are colored similarly to the adults. The head and body length is 20–22 mm, the tail 25–27 mm. They may be fed with small wax moth larvae, crickets, and fruitflies. Juvenile deaths are infrequent, and even the weakest individuals soon develop into robust specimens. They are sexually mature and almost as large at their parents at 18 months of age.

The male is distinguished from the female by the presence of prominent pre-anal tubercles and a thickened tail-base. In the female the pre-anal tubercles are poorly developed and the tail base is relatively slender.

The males of this species can be aggressive to each other, and one may bite the other in the neck or the tail. This does not result in serious injuries, but it can cause psychological stress symptoms. This small and interesting gecko is suitable for the beginner.

Chondrodactylus angulifer Sand Gecko

RANGE: Southern Namibia (Greater Namaqualand), southwestern Botswana, and the Republic of South Africa (central, western, northwestern, and northern parts of Cape Province).

HABITAT: This terrestrial species is at home in sandy desert and savannah regions. During the day it hides in burrows of scorpions or rodents.

DESCRIPTION: This is a robust gecko that reaches a total length of 172 mm. The massive head is markedly set off from the body. The slightly whorled tail is round in section.

The granular scales of the upper side are interspersed with large tubercular scales on the back of the head, the back, the tail, and the limbs. On the back these are arranged in rows. Above the eyes are large scales that probably protect them from sand. A similar function is performed by the small nostrils and the long, narrow ear openings. The feet are also adapted for a life in the sand— the short toes are provided with rows of spine-like scales that form a comb-like grip for moving over the substrate. Such an adaptation is seen in many desert-dwelling lizard species.

The coloration of this species is extremely variable and ranges from yellowish brown to reddish brown, which matches the color of the substrate in its particular habitat. While some specimens may be uniformly colored and poorly marked, the majority show three or four brown-bordered transverse brown bands on the back, the anterior one darkest. A light gray to light brown stripe extends on the side of the head from the back of the eye to meet (or nearly so) in the middle of the neck with the stripe from the other side. This stripe is also bordered in brown. The underside is plain white.

In contrast to most other gecko species, *C. angulifer* exhibits marked sexual dimorphism. The base of the tail is thicker in the male than in the

Adult female Sand Gecko, *Chondrodactylus angulifer*. This is a well-marked specimen. Photo by P. v. d. Elzen, courtesy Dr. D. Terver, Nancy Aquarium, France.

A gravid female Southern Leaf-tailed Gecko, *Phyllurus platurus*, from Australia. The flat tail and irregularly colored body aid the gecko in hiding on the side of trees. Photo by K. H. Switak.

female. At the sides of the tail vertical hook-like scales are more strongly developed in the male. The female possesses tiny withdrawable claws on the toes of her hind feet. Males also have a difference in color pattern, having one to four brown-bordered white blotches along each flank (absent or weak in females).

BIOLOGY, CARE, AND BREEDING: A simple, dry terrarium about 50 x 40 x 40 cm in size is suitable for two or three specimens. Yellow or reddish sand is most suitable as substrate material. Hiding places can consist of piles of stones (preferably cemented together), pieces of bark, earthenware tiles and tubes, and artificial rocks made of styrofoam. The hiding places must be made so that the animals can comfortably stand with their legs outstretched. Planting of the terrarium is not essential nor is a drinking vessel, but regular spraying is necessary.

Although this species comes from the Southern Hemisphere, it adapts well to our terrarium conditions. For the first year, however, you should respect the climatic requirements of a newly imported animal. Daytime temperatures can be 30°C or more. As these geckos like to have a warm belly, it is recommended that the substrate be heated. A few spots can reach

35°C, but it is important that cooler areas are also available. At night the heating apparatus should be switched off to allow a natural fall in temperature. When the light is switched off the geckos will leave their hiding places and go hunting for food. They are pretty voracious and in the wild will eat spiders, scorpions, and other geckos (*Colopus wahlbergii*) as well as insects (termites, beetles, moths, crickets). They are not suitable for community terraria with other gecko species. In the

Facing page: This female New Zealand Green Gecko, *Naultinus elegans*, is preparing to drop to another branch. Judging from the condition of the abdomen, she may be gravid. Photo by K. H. Switak.

Bibron's Gecko, *Pachydactylus bibroni*, is common in southern Africa, large (20 cm), eats well, and is long-lived. They make excellent pets and are bred in captivity. Photo by Kenneth T. Nemuras.

Left: The Sand Gecko, *Chondrodactylus angulifer angulifer*, exhibits obvious sexual dimorphism in color pattern as well as tail shape. The male (lower photo) has brown-bordered whitish ocelli on each side of the midline, though the number varies. Photos by H. Rosler.

Below: One of the most distinctive geckos is the Helmeted Gecko, *Geckonia chazaliae*, which has a row of large spines at the back of the head as in some American horned lizards. It is from northern Africa. Photo by K. H. Switak.

terrarium they may be fed a variety of crickets, cockroaches, and wax moths and their larvae.

It is possible to breed this species in the terrarium. Even the eggs laid by freshly imported females can be incubated and hatched. Females can lay up to four clutches in a short time (every 10–11 days). The very thin-shelled eggs are buried in the substrate by the female. In the wild, gravid females may be found from September to January; newly hatched young are present from December to March. The incubation period is therefore probably in the region of two to three months. In the terrarium the 68 mm young hatch in 57–91 days (with an incubation temperature of 20–30°C and a relative air humidity nearing 100%).

The color pattern of the juvenile Sand Geckos is only marginally different from that of the adults, but the colors, as with most gecko species, have greater contrast. Rearing of these young geckos should pose no difficulty.

The Sand Gecko can be regarded as a long-lived terrestrial species, having lived in captivity for more than six years. Continual breeding over several generations is not easy, and the species therefore is recommended only for experienced herpetologists.

Crossobamon eversmanni
Comb-toed Gecko

RANGE: Southern USSR (from the Caspian Sea and southern Kazakhstan to Tjan-Schan), northwestern Afghanistan, and northern Iran.

HABITAT: Inhabits semi-desert areas with sand dunes and medium height vegetation. In some areas it shares its habitat with the Wonder Gecko, *Teratoscincus scincus*. Like that species, it makes burrows in the sand up to 80 cm in length. At the end of the burrow it enlarges a living space. It probably also utilizes the burrows of beetles and rodents, making itself an annex to the main burrow.

DESCRIPTION: The Comb-toed Gecko is built more like a typical lizard than a gecko. It has a large triangular head mounted on a relatively slender body that runs into a fine, tapered tail. The limbs are long and thin and enable the reptile to walk high-legged across the hot sand in the evenings. The long, thin tail is also used as an aid to climbing in the vegetation.

The ground color of this species matches exactly the color of the sand in its habitat and varies from light brown to ocher. The head, body, and limbs are set with small, irregular brown patches and spots. A brown stripe extends from the rear of the eye to roughly one-third of the way between the fore and rear limbs. The tail is brown-banded on the upper side, while the underside is plainly colored.

The body is covered with small, granular scales except for three rows of enlarged scales on each side of the spine.

The name Comb-toed Gecko comes from the rows of comb-like scales on the toes that help the reptile to move through fine sand. The ear openings are vertical and narrow to keep the sand out. The relatively large eyes are graced with vertical, slightly scalloped pupils.

The total length of this species is 10 cm, of which 6 cm is taken up by the tail.

BIOLOGY, CARE, AND BREEDING: A dry terrarium with dimensions of 40 x 30 x 30 cm is adequate for a pair of these geckos. The substrate should consist of a layer of sand 5–6 cm deep, one part of which is kept damp for egg-laying. Cork bark, a many-branched twig, and a clump of tall grass will complete the furnishings. The temperature requirements are the same as those of the Wonder Gecko. The usual insects can be supplied for food, but the geckos seem to prefer slow-moving insects.

This species is difficult to obtain, but it should breed if kept in the conditions described for *Teratoscincus scincus*. The eggs of wild-caught females have been successfully incubated.

The female lays one or two 12 mm eggs in June/July, burying them in the sand. At an incubation temperature of 25–30°C, the 54–59 mm young will hatch in 45–53 days. Apart from an orange-red color under the tail, the juveniles resemble the adults in color. They may be reared on very small insects. This species is suitable for the more experienced herpetologist.

Cyrtodactylus kotschyi
Kotschy's Gecko, Aegean Bow-fingered Gecko

RANGE: Southeastern Italy, southern Balkan Peninsula (southern Jugoslavia, Albania, Greece, Bulgaria), the Ionian and Aegean Islands, Cyprus, and southwestern Asia (southern Turkey, Syria, Lebanon, and Israel).

HABITAT: This species inhabits many different habitats including stone piles, stone walls, low vegetation, cactus clumps, buildings, and trees. These habitats are not always used at the same time, and there are ecological influences (other lizard species present, etc.). While it is mainly found in vegetation on the islands, it seems to prefer buildings on the mainland. In Israel and Turkey it lives on trees and under loose bark.

DESCRIPTION: This gecko is able to physically change color and, as there is a great variation in the range, it is difficult to lay down hard and fast rules (there are over 20 subspecies described) regarding a characteristic color and pattern.

The ground color is mainly light gray to dark gray, but there are populations where this is yellowish, orange, reddish, or dark brown. There are six or seven dark transverse bands along the back that also run into the neck and the limbs. Next to the dark bands are broken bands consisting of white to light gray flecks. The upper side of the tail is also furnished with light

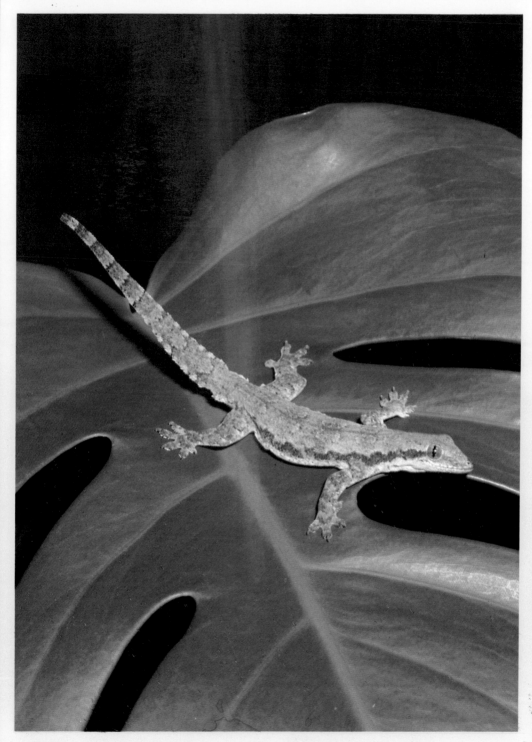

Cosymbotus craspedotus, the common Thai House Gecko. Photo by K. H. Switak.

and dark bands. The belly is white, and the underside of the (unregenerated) tail is yellow.

The wide, flat head is set off distinctly from the neck and covered with tiny granular scales sprinkled with larger keeled scales. There are 8–14 longitudinal rows of tubercular scales along the back that are surrounded by small granular scales. Large tubercular scales are also set among the granular scales of the upper sides of the limbs. The belly is covered with large, flat scales (20–40 longitudinal rows in the middle of the body) that are notched at the posterior side. The tail has 17–24 transverse rows of scales, each containing 4–6 tubercular scales.

Kotschy's Gecko reaches a total length of 135 mm but is commonly in the region of 100 mm. The ratio of head and body length to tail length varies between 0.80–0.85 : 1.5–1.20.

BIOLOGY, CARE, AND BREEDING: This little gecko does not have high demands for its housing. A terrarium with dimensions of 50 x 40 x 40 cm is adequate for four or five specimens. Sand can be used as the substrate, but a corner (kept moist) should be mixed with a little potting

Cyrtodactylus pulchellus, the Malayan Bow-fingered or Jewel Gecko, a species that requires cool, humid environments. Photo by Burkhard Kahl.

compost. On the back wall or in the center of the substrate a secure pile of stones with plenty of hiding places should be provided. A decorative twig and a shallow water dish will complete the furnishings.

In its natural habitat this species is often abroad during the day, especially in the mornings and late afternoons, when they bask in the sun and take on a dark color. The main activity time, however, is at dusk and through the night. At these times its color is much lighter.

This species is very fond of sun and warmth, and it has been

Although it often is placed in the genus *Phyllurus* along with the leaf-tailed geckos, most herpetologists put this gecko in its own genus as *Underwoodisaurus milii* from Australia. Photo by Robert S. Simmons.

seen basking at a temperature of 50°C (measured in the sun). The optimal temperature for these geckos is around 42°C. Such a high temperature in the terrarium can be accomplished with a heat lamp. Broad-spectrum fluorescent tubes are recommended for general lighting. The air temperature

during the day should be maintained at 28–35°C, and the optimal temperature should be available in part of the terrarium for at least a few hours daily. At night the temperature should be lowered to 22–24°C. The daily light cycle should be seasonally varied to suit that of the Northern Hemisphere. Hibernation is not necessary, but winter daytime temperatures should be reduced to 25°C, 18°C at night.

The high temperatures tolerated by these geckos indicate a high rate of metabolism, and they are incapable of going for long without food (in contrast to most other gecko species). Adult specimens must be fed well at least every two to three days. Newly hatched and growing juveniles must be fed daily, otherwise losses will occur.

They will eat spiders, crickets, grasshoppers, small moths, beetles, mealworms, houseflies, woodlice, and cockroaches. Many keepers of this species

The Web-footed Gecko, *Palmatogecko rangei*, is one of the many herpetological wonders of the Namib Desert. This delicate burrower is readily recognized by the webbed feet and the large, blood-shot eyes. Photos by Paul Freed.

have noted that they tend to suffer from paralysis even when fed a highly varied diet. By adding a calcium supplement to the food insects and vitamin D_3 to the drinking water, this problem can be surmounted, but it must be guarded against.

The breeding season begins in spring (April/May). The male bites the female's neck and holds her tightly while maneuvering his tail under hers to complete copulation. Depending on the natural range, egg-laying begins in May and continues into late summer (August). The young hatch from July to October after an incubation period of 78–83 days. Usually two eggs (8–11 x 7–9 mm) are laid, sometimes one. The eggs are laid under stones, in stone walls, etc., but are sometimes also buried in loose earth.

The newly hatched young have a head/body length of 17–19 mm and a tail length of 19 mm. In contrast to the adults, the tails of juveniles are yellow to orange-yellow on the dorsal surface.

It is difficult to determine the sexes in this species as there is no notable dimorphism. The males are generally smaller than females, but the difference is so small that it can only be determined by examining a large number of specimens. The examination of the post-anal

Afroedura transvaalica, the Transvaal Fat Gecko of southern Africa. Photo by K. H. Switak.

The Cat Gecko, *Aeluroscalabotes felinus*, a Southeast Asian eyelid gecko that may be one of the most primitive living geckos. Photo by M. J. Cox.

region (the base of the tail just behind the vent) can help. In the male the inverted hemipenes form an angular shape and there are also 2–9 pre-anal pores. In rare cases, females also have pre-anal pores. Given adequate warmth and a varied diet, Kotschy's Gecko is a fine terrarium subject. It has lived in captivity for six years.

Cyrtodactylus caspius
Caspian Bow-fingered Gecko

RANGE: From the northwestern coast of the Caspian Sea through southern USSR and northern and eastern Iran to northwestern Afghanistan.

HABITAT: In its natural habitat this species may be terrestrial or arboreal and is often found around human habitation. It colonizes loess and limestone walls, ravines, and ruins, also sometimes trees and rodent burrows.

DESCRIPTION: This species has a total length of 163 mm (ratio of head/body to tail length 1:1.2). The ground color of the upper side is composed of light gray or brownish gray shades. Five or six irregular transverse dark brown bands extend from the neck along the back; a further 10–12 bands are on the tail. The underside of the body is a uniform white.

The slightly flattened body is clad in granular and tubercular scales, and the relatively large head is covered with small, smooth, granular scales. From

the toes that do not allow this species to scale smooth, glassy surfaces.

The eye is well developed and possesses a vertical pupil with four openings. The narrow ear openings are distinctly visible.

Both the males and the females possess 23–28 pre-anal pores, but these are only active

Cyrtodactylus louisiadensis, an attractive bow-fingered gecko. Photo by R. D. Bartlett.

the rear of the head and along the back to the ventral region extend 12–16 longitudinal rows of large, keeled, tubercular scales that are surrounded by smaller granular scales. The whorled tail is beset with large spine-like scales.

There are smooth subdigital lamellae on the undersides of

in the male, where they are brown and swollen. In the female these pores are poorly developed. This is a good method of sex determination.

BIOLOGY, CARE, AND BREEDING: In the wild this species hibernates from October to March, but in the terrarium a four-week winter rest period at 12–15°C is sufficient. Captive breeding behavior has not yet been observed, but in the wild, gravid females have been found in April and May. In the terrarium egg-laying can occur earlier, perhaps as early as February. A second clutch may be produced in August to October. Two hard-shelled eggs (8–10 x 12–15 mm), sometimes one, occur in a clutch.

In the wild, the young hatch from the end of June until the late fall. Eggs incubated in a 10 x 10 cm plastic box lined with slightly moist filter paper and kept at a daytime temperature of 25–27°C and a nighttime temperature of 18–20°C will hatch in 68–81 days. The newly hatched young have a head/body length of 23–26 mm. Color and pattern are similar to adults but perhaps somewhat richer in contrast. They have a relatively larger head and limbs and a shorter tail than the adults.

Care, breeding, and rearing of this species should pose few problems. One male and four females can be kept in a 50 x 40 x 40 cm terrarium furnished as described for *Cyrtodactylus*

One of the prettiest bow-fingered geckos is *Cyrtodactylus peguensis*, often available from Thailand. Photo by Kenneth T. Nemuras.

Like other *Cyrtodactylus* species, the Thai Bow-fingered Gecko requires relatively high humidities and cooler nighttime temperatures. Photo by Kenneth T. Nemuras.

kotschyi. A daytime temperature of 28–30°C (locally to 35°C) can be reduced to 20–22°C at night.

Cyrtodactylus peguensis
Thai Bow-fingered Gecko

RANGE: Southeastern Burma (town of Pegu) to southern Thailand.

HABITAT: Lives in jungle regions along the banks of rivers and streams. During the day it takes refuge in hollow tree limbs or under leaf litter.

DESCRIPTION: The ground color of this species ranges from light to dark brown with a very variable pattern of darker brown flecks. A short dark stripe stretches from the rear of the eye to just above the ear opening. In some specimens the stripes and flecks run into each other so that a fork-like stripe runs from the eye to the neck, across the body and back to the other eye. A series of seven or eight pairs of dark brown oval patches runs from the shoulder to the base of the tail. These are flanked on both sides by a row of dark brown bars that merge into the underside. The unregenerated tail is patterned with black and white bands, the seven white bands being broken with irregular black spots. The regenerated tail is plain light to dark gray, with no pattern. The underside is yellowish white.

The body is covered with small granular scales interspersed with larger (three times as large) flat, slightly keeled tubercular scales. The head is relatively large and wider than the round body at its thickest spot.

C. peguensis can reach a total length of 130 mm; the head/body to tail ratio is 1:1. Regenerated tails are usually shorter.

The male can be easily distinguished from the female by his thickened tailbase caused by inverted hemipenes.

BIOLOGY, CARE, AND BREEDING: Although this beautiful gecko is frequently imported, we do not know much about it. Captive breeding has not yet been reported, although egg-laying has been observed.

Unfortunately, due to the Thai dealers' ignorance of the humidity requirements of this species, they arrive in very bad condition. Losses during transportation are alarmingly high, and more than 50–60% of imported specimens can be lost. Those that arrive in reasonable condition, however, can soon be revived in a humid terrarium.

A terrarium of the type used for tropical frogs is ideal for this gecko species. Loose woodland earth or a mixture of peat and potting compost can be used for the substrate. A hollow branch is important so the geckos can seek out a dry refuge. The terrarium can be spartanly planted with a few climbing plants (*Scindapsus, pothos*) or thickly planted with such species as stagshorn fern, croton, etc. Stones are not

Cyrtodactylus species. There are numerous bow-fingered geckos and many species are difficult or impossible to identify. Photo by Robert S. Simmons.

Like *Cyrtodactylus peguensis*, *C. pulchellus* requires high humidities and cool nighttime temperatures. This species recently has bred in captivity and may become more widely available. Photos by Kenneth T. Nemuras.

necessary, but a few branches are decorative and will increase the climbing area for the geckos.

The temperature in the terrarium (50 x 40 x 40 cm) should be maintained at 28–32°C during the day, reduced to 23–25°C at night. Relative air humidity should be 70–100%.

You are unlikely to observe much of the behavior of these geckos as, like some other tropical species (*Cyrtodactylus deccanensis*, *Eublepharis kuroiwae*, etc.), they are strictly nocturnal and only emerge to hunt when it is totally dark.

RELATED SPECIES: Of the many colorful Southeast Asian species in this genus, the Malayan Bow-finger (*Cyrtodactylus pulchellus*) is regularly imported. It is found in northeastern India (Bengal), Burma, Thailand, and Malaysia. Growing to nearly 260 mm (head/body 115 mm, tail 144 mm), it is a species from mountainous areas (over 1300 m), where it lives on trees, rock faces, and in hollows, also occasionally in human habitations. Care is as for *C. peguensis*, but the temperature should not exceed 26°C, reduced to 22–23°C at night.

Gekko gecko
Tokay Gecko

RANGE: Northeastern India and Bangladesh, Burma, Thailand, Indochina, southern China, Malaysia, Malaysian Archipelago, Indonesia, Philippines, Sulu Archipelago, and the eastern Indo-Australasian Archipelago.

HABITAT: Although originally an inhabitant of the tropical rain forest, it has begun to colonize human habitations.

DESCRIPTION: This large, 25 cm, aggressive gecko has attractive

The large mouth and aggressive posture of the Tokay Gecko, *Gekko gecko*, are perhaps its most prominent features. Photo by Burkhard Kahl.

coloration. The gray to blue ground color is strewn with orange to red spots and flecks. The large head is covered with small angular scales, and the body is covered with small granular scales in which rows of tubercular scales are embedded. The toes are provided with large, undivided adhesive pads. The male is distinguished from the female by an angular row of 10–24 pre-anal pores.

BIOLOGY, CARE, AND BREEDING: In its natural habitat the Tokay is well-known for its vocalization. Starting with a call not unlike the cackling of a hen, it will break into a series of "to-kay, to-kay" sounds that give it its common name. The call ends with clucking tones that are not unlike laughter. These calls are designed to help the geckos find mates in the breeding season. Only the males make the "to-kay" call; however, the females make do with a short croaking call. Normally the call is made only in the evenings and at night, but it occasionally may be heard during the daylight hours.

Tokay geckos are full of fight and, should an enemy approach, will open their broad mouths wide. If this should fail to scare the aggressor, they will bite strongly. As these bites can be quite painful, it is best to wear strong gloves when handling this species.

A large, high terrarium (minimum 80 x 50 x 100 cm) is required for a male and two or three females. Strong plants such as croton, *Sanseveria,*

A recent fad involves the use of Tokay Geckos to control cockroaches in New York apartments. Dryness, cool temperatures, and pesticides make this dangerous for the lizard. Photo by H. Hansen.

The scientific name of the Tokay, *Gekko gecko*, often confuses amateurs, who believe the two names should be spelled the same. *Gekko* is the correct spelling of the generic name, while *gecko* is correct for the specific name. Photo by Kenneth T. Nemuras.

Hoya (wax flower), etc., are recommended. The back wall of the terrarium should be lined with bark or split branches. A potting compost/sand mixture should be used for substrate. A few strong branches and one or two cork bark tubes will complete the furnishings. A large, shallow dish of drinking water should be provided.

The terrarium interior should be sprayed once or twice each day so that the daytime relative humidity does not drop below 50-60%. At nighttime it can reach 80-90%. Being a tropical species, the Tokay requires a daytime temperature of 27–35°C,

somewhat warmer under the heat lamp. A temperature of 22–25°C is adequate at night.

Anyone deciding to keep Tokays should ensure a constant, reliable source of food. Without breeding colonies of food insects, you will fail. A richly varied diet seems to be important to bring the reptiles into breeding condition, and they can devour surprising amounts. The Tokay will devour anything it can overcome, so it can be provided with locusts, large crickets, and even baby mice as well as the usual food insects.

The Tokay frequently has been

bred in captivity. The females lay several clutches of two hard-shelled eggs per year. The eggs adhere to the laying surface, usually one above the other. A warm dark spot in the terrarium, sometimes on the wall or on a climbing branch, is chosen as a laying site. Incubation time varies from 100 to 182 days. Newly hatched juveniles are 10 cm long.

As the eggs cannot be removed from the terrarium without damage (unless the laying surface is removed with them), they should be protected with a little mesh cage until they hatch. Observations in the terrarium have revealed that the male

Eyes often are the most prominent feature of a gecko and are worth a careful study. The pupils have several obvious scallops at the margins, readily visible in the Tokay above. Since most geckos with vertical pupils are nocturnal, it is believed that the pinholes or scallops aid in reducing glare during any daytime activity. Note that in the Tokay on the facing page the pupil has contracted to just a thin line with obvious pinholes where the scallops come together. Photo above by Burkhard Kahl, that on facing page by Kenneth T. Nemuras.

Tokay will guard the eggs and newly hatched young. The black-and-white-banded juveniles can be reared with small food items in the same container as their parents, but it is perhaps safer to remove them to a separate container. Provided with a rich variety of foods, the young will be almost fully grown in 12 months and sexually mature shortly afterward.

Given adequate warmth and food, the Tokay is an interesting, long-living terrarium subject that is recommended for the beginner.

Facing page: Smith's Green-eyed Gecko, *Gekko smithii*, recognizable by the emerald green eye. Many geckos appear emaciated even under natural conditions. Photo above by R. G. Sprackland, that below by M. J. Cox.

A group of Tokay Geckos. The rust-red spots are distinctive. Photo by H. Hansen.

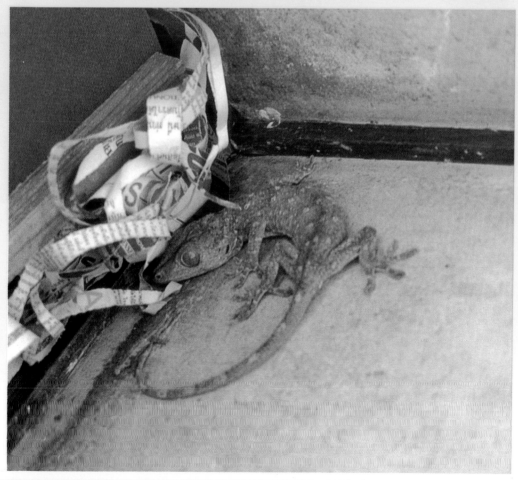

RELATED SPECIES: In addition to the Tokay, Smith's Green-eyed Gecko (*G. smithii*) and the Great Malayan House Gecko (*G. monarchus*) are occasionally imported.

Gekko smithii is found in Burma, Thailand, the Andaman and Nicobar Islands, Malaysia, and the islands of the Indo-Australasian Archipelago. It is a large (up to 370 mm) tree-dwelling and nocturnal species. It is less likely to be found near human habitations than the Tokay. The body color is gray, brownish gray, or greenish white. The back is decorated with regular rows of white and dark brown spots. The green eyes with the vertical pupils with multiple openings give this species its common name.

Terrarium, temperature, and diet are as described for the Tokay, although the terrarium should be more thickly planted and the humidity somewhat higher. Captive breeding has not yet been accomplished.

The Great Malayan House Gecko ranges from southern

Gekko vittatus, perhaps one of the most distinctive of the Tokay group. Because genera of lizards are based on morphological characters (such as structure of the feet, scalation of the head and body, and bone structure) and not on color patterns, very different-looking species may be in the same genus, while geckos with superficially identical color patterns may be in unrelated genera. Photo by R. D. Bartlett.

Thailand through Malaysia and the Indo-Australasian Archipelago to the Philippines. It grows to a total length of over 200 mm. In its range, it is sometimes found in human habitations that are in jungle or close to its margins.

The ground color is brown. Nine or ten small, irregular dark brown to black pairs of patches extend from the neck to the beginning of the tail. Similar but not so obvious patches extend along the tail, forming incomplete rings.

This species also requires a warm, humid terrarium. Breeding is possible. The two hard-shelled eggs (13.35 x 10.20 mm) are stuck to the laying surface or simply laid on the substrate. They hatch in 92–100 days. It is suspected that *G. monarchus* is not averse to devouring its own offspring, so the eggs should be removed for incubation or protected with a mesh cage. The juveniles should be reared in separate accommodations.

Both sexes possess pre-anal pores set in an angular

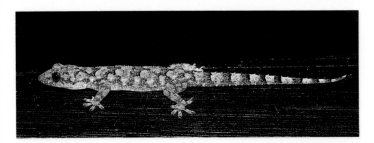

Hemidactylus mabouia, one of the numerous species of *Hemidactylus* found in Africa. Species of this genus are difficult to distinguish. Photo by Dr. Guido Dingerkus.

arrangement; those of the female are smaller and poorly developed.

Hemidactylus turcicus
Turkish Gecko

RANGE: This species has a very wide range of distribution. It is found on the coasts around the Mediterranean and on most Mediterranean islands, along the coasts of the Red Sea, and in the Middle East as far as Sind and Pakistan. It also has colonized parts of North and Central America (southern USA, Mexico, Panama) and the Caribbean area (Cuba, Puerto Rico) as well as the Canary Islands.

HABITAT: *H. turcicus* seems to have no great restrictions regarding its habitat. It is found in houses, ruins, and stone walls as well as cliffs, caves, rabbit burrows, and under tree trunks. In America it even lives

Hemidactylus persicus from Pakistan. Although many *Hemidactylus* live around humans and are carried about by accident, others are seldom introduced into foreign countries. Photo by Dr. Sherman Minton.

in bromeliads.

DESCRIPTION: The Turkish Gecko can reach a total length of 123 mm, but European specimens are usually fully grown in the region of 100 mm. The nearly round tail makes up a little more than half the total length.

It is a slimly built species. The flattish head is set off prominently from the body. The back is covered with granular scales interspersed with large tubercles on the back of the head, the back, limbs, and upper tail. The tubercles on the back are strongly keeled and arranged in 14–16 longitudinal rows; those on the tail are somewhat spine-like. The regenerated tail is adorned only with small granular scales. The subcaudal scales are wide and are arranged somewhat in the manner of the belly scales of a snake.

There are numerous variations of color and pattern. The ground color can range from yellowish white through yellowish brown (sand color) to brownish pink or reddish gray. The pattern is formed from irregular brown to dark brown patches that are the remnants of the juvenile banded pattern. In adults, the tail bands can still be perceived with

One of the more distinctively patterned *Hemidactylus* species, *Hemidactylus triedrus* from the Indian subcontinent. Photo by Dr. Sherman Minton.

Unidentified *Hemidactylus* sometimes are imported. Unless there is information to the contrary, they probably can be kept much like Turkish Geckos.

Above: A fairly typical Turkish Gecko, *Hemidactylus turcicus*. Compare this specimen with the one on the facing page. Photo by E. Zimmermann. Below: *Hemiphyllodactylus typus*, one of several Pacific Island geckos widely introduced by commerce. Photo by S. McKeown and G. K. Uchida.

Although the pattern of this Turkish Gecko is weak, you can still see the brown and white spotting typical of the species. The large tubercles on the lower sides are distinctive, as is the relatively long and pointed snout. Turkish Geckos sometimes tend to fade to almost ghost-like shades at night when hunting under bright outdoor lights. Photo by Kenneth T. Nemuras.

difficulty. A narrow brown stripe (sometimes barely discernible) extends from the snout through the eye to the ear opening. During the day this species is much darker than at night, when it can be almost white.

BIOLOGY, CARE, AND BREEDING: In the summer months the Turkish Gecko is crepuscular and nocturnal. Its main activity time is evenings and early nights. In spring and fall it may be observed abroad during the daylight hours. It often is attracted to insects at lights.

In the terrarium, this species will usually start searching for food after the lights go out. They will take crickets, grasshoppers, flies, spiders, moths, mealworms, and wax moth larvae. With regular spraying, a drinking vessel is unnecessary.

Information on the breeding behavior of this species is available, but some details still are unknown. For example, it is not known when European specimens begin to pair. I was able to observe my pair copulating on April 16 at 2315 hours. The smaller male took the female in his jaws just behind her ear opening. The tails were not intertwined. The female raised her tail so that the male could bring his cloaca into contact with hers. Copulation took three to four minutes.

The females produce four or even five clutches of two hard-shelled eggs (9-11 x 10 x 13 mm) during the breeding season. Occasionally a clutch consists of one or three eggs. The eggs are laid in crevices or cavities in rocks or walls, where they are concealed under earth and sparse vegetation. In the wild, incubation periods of 6-12 weeks have been suggested, but in captivity the young will hatch in 41-50 days at an incubation temperature of 28-31°C. The incubator should have a relative air humidity of nearly 100% (although 60-70% is adequate).

As with eggs of the Wall Gecko, the incubation medium must remain dry and the eggs must not come into contact with water. The eggs should not be buried on the substrate; it is adequate to lay them on the surface.

Newly hatched juveniles have a head/body length of 24-27 mm, the tail being just as long or a little longer. The youngsters are marked differently from their parents. The basic shade is flesh to light brown. Five wide dark brown bands extend along the back, merging into the flanks in a "U" formation. A weak broken band traverses the neck. Eleven or 12 dark and light bands decorate the tail, becoming more intense toward the tip. The light bands may be light gray, light brown, or white, the dark ones dark brown to black. The belly is whitish and somewhat transparent.

Rearing of the young is simple, and they are nearly fully grown and sexually mature at just over one year of age. The young can be reared with their parents at first as the adults do not attack them, but when the young males

The large lateral (side) tubercles are very prominent on the Turkish Gecko in this photo, as are the more widely spaced and somewhat pointed tubercles on the tail. *Hemidactylus turcicus* is a type of animal often called a synanthrope; that is, it often is found associated with human dwellings and possessions. Because it is small, tough enough to survive long journeys by sea, and lays hard-shelled eggs that will survive under difficult conditions attached to plants and even pieces of pottery, it is easily spread by commerce. Once in a suitable area where winter temperatures are not too low, it is able to reproduce and become fairly common if it has little competition. Photo by Kenneth T. Nemuras.

Above: Eggs of geckos often are enormous in relation to the size of the parent. The two eggs of this Turkish Gecko weigh a good percentage of the adult's weight, yet this female might produce four more clutches during a good year. Photo by Robert S. Simmons.

Facing page: Captive breeding leads to stabilized color variants. Albinistic Turkish Geckos (contrasted with a normally patterned specimen) can now be produced in fair numbers if desired. Photo by Bertrand E. Baur.

reach sexual maturity they must be removed or they will be attacked and bitten by their father. The male is distinguished from the female by the presence of strongly developed pre-anal pores and post-cloacal scales. Males tend to have wider heads than females.

The Turkish Gecko has a loud voice that is used to indicate territoriality. In the terrarium it also has been observed that the call is part of the breeding behavior.

A terrarium setup as described for *Cyrtodactylus kotschyi* is suitable for a pair of Turkish Geckos. A daylight fluorescent tube and a 40 watt tungsten bulb are adequate for heating and lighting. Daytime temperatures should be in the region of 30-32°C, reduced to 22-24°C at night. It is useful to adjust the lighting for seasonal variations. A six to eight weeks winter rest period at reduced temperatures will prepare the geckos for breeding.

RELATED SPECIES: The Indian House Gecko, *Hemidactylus flaviviridis,* is occasionally imported. The range of this plainly colored, 15-cm species extends from coastal areas of East Africa (Somalia, Ethiopia, Sudan) over the Arabian Peninsula, through Iraq, Iran, Pakistan, and southeastern Afghanistan, across northern India to Bangladesh.

It is common around human habitations and, like *H. turcicus,* is mainly crepuscular and nocturnal. Its captive requirements are similar to those of the Turkish Gecko.

The ground color of the Indian House Gecko varies from light gray to yellowish brown with a darker marbling on the back.

The body is covered with small granular scales. Large tubercular scales occur only on the tail.

In the breeding season the female produces up to three clutches of two 12 mm hard-shelled eggs. The eggs are not buried and require an incubation temperature of 26°C and a relative humidity of 50-60%, when they will take about 62 days to hatch. The juveniles are easy to rear but must be separated from the adults.

The Chit-chat or Pale House Gecko *(Hemidactylus frenatus)* is another species of house gecko that, originating in Southeast Asia, has developed a wide distribution and occurs in Pakistan, Nepal, India, Sri Lanka, the Andaman, Nicobar, and Maldive Islands, Indochina, southern China, Taiwan, Japan (Okinawa Island), the Philippines, and the Sulu and Indo-Australasian Archipelagos. In addition, it has colonized New Guinea, northern Australia, Oceania, Mexico, eastern Africa (Somalia), Madagascar and neighboring islands, Mauritius, and South Africa.

H. frenatus is a slender and very agile species that, in addition to houses, lives on palm trees, on rocky outcrops, and under stones. The total length is some 120 mm, of which about half is taken up by the narrow tail. There are six longitudinal rows of cone-shaped scales on the tail. The body is covered with small granular scales dotted here and there with larger

A gravid Chit-chat, *Hemidactylus frenatus*. The two eggs are easily visible through the translucent abdominal skin. Photo by S. McKeown.

This *Hemidactylus mabouia* is using its tongue to clean its eye. Because eyelids are absent in most geckos, this is a common behavior. However, even eyelid geckos use the tongue to clean their eyes. Photo by Kenneth T. Nemuras.

tubercles. The back is yellowish brown to grayish brown in color. Sometimes two dark longitudinal stripes are present along the upper flanks. These are dotted with tiny lighter patches. In some specimens a further dark stripe runs from the snout through the eye to the neck. During the night this species takes on a uniformly whitish color.

The Chit-chat requires husbandry similar to other *Hemidactylus* species. In contrast to these, however, it will show itself in the daytime, sometimes basking under the heat lamp.

The female lays two hard-shelled eggs that will hatch in 47-55 days at an incubation temperature of 32°C. The juveniles are 46-50 mm in length.

Heteronotia binoei
Bynoe's Gecko

RANGE: Australia, with the exception of the wet southwestern (West Australia) and southeastern (New South Wales) regions.

HABITAT: *H. binoei* inhabits varied biotopes, from damp coastal forests to desert areas. It is mainly terrestrial and seeks refuge behind loose bark, in rock crevices, and under fallen timber.

DESCRIPTION: This small species has a head/body length of 50 mm and a round tail of 35-40 mm. The body is covered with fine granular scales among which numerous tubercles are scattered. Sometimes the tubercular scales are arranged in rows. One such row contains 25 tubercles.

The color is very variable, ranging from light brown and reddish brown through light gray to black. It typically has numerous irregularly distributed white, yellow, and brown spots and flecks. These markings sometimes can be so arranged as to form broken tranverse

bands across the body. A brown or gray streak extends from the tip of the snout through the eye to the back of the head.

BIOLOGY, CARE, AND BREEDING: *H. binoei* is mainly nocturnal and hunts a variety of small insects and spiders. Sometimes it will appear in the terrarium during the day and bask under the heat lamp.

Male and female are similar in color and pattern, but males can be distinguished by the pre-anal pores. The females have calcium deposits in the throat region.

One or two eggs (9.5 x 6.5 mm) are laid up to four times per year. These can be up to 30% of the body weight of the female. At an incubation temperature of 26-29°C and a relative humidity of 50%, the

Lepidodactylus lugubris, the Scaly-fingered Gecko, also is known as the Mourning Gecko because of its somber colors. Photo by S. McKeown.

young will hatch in about 68 days. The juveniles weigh 0.2 g and are 35-40 mm in length. They may be reared easily on fruitflies, small crickets, and wax moth larvae.

This species requires a small dry terrarium (30 x 25 x 25 cm) with a sandy substrate and a few pieces of bark as refuges. Such a setup is suitable for a male and two or three females. Provide daytime temperatures from 28-32°C, with a local temperature to 35°C. At night the temperature can be reduced to about 20°C. Lighting should be not less than 12 hours per day. A daily spraying is recommended. This little gecko is very suitable for beginners.

Lepidodactylus lugubris
Scaly-fingered Gecko, Mourning Gecko

RANGE: Ceylon (Sri Lanka), Nicobar and Andaman Islands, Malayan Peninsula, Indo-Australasian Archipelago, Philippines, Oceania (Tahiti, New Caledonia, Hawaii, etc.). Introduced into New Zealand (Mokohinau Islands, Hauraki Gulf), the western coast of Central America (Panama Canal Zone), and northern South America.

HABITAT: The Scaly-finger, as can be seen from its range, has a varied habitat and is very adaptable. It may be found on beaches under the bark of driftwood and in the leaf axils of palms, as well as in human habitations.

DESCRIPTION: At 80 mm total length, more than half being taken up by the tail, *L. lugubris* is one of the smaller gecko species.

The toes are only marginally widened, and each carries two rows of reddish adhesive lamellae. The fifth toe carries a tiny claw.

The color can change with temperature and mood. At high temperatures (30°C) and when startled, it shows a sallow beige ground color with a double row of black or brown spots stretching from the neck to the tail-base. At lower temperatures (20°C) the ground color becomes brown or dark gray with darker wavy bands arranged along the body and tail. Juveniles also show these bands on a light brown background. The flanks and the limbs are dark brown and contrast strongly with the pattern of the back and tail.

It is quite possible that these geckos are able to change color to suit their immediate surroundings. It is sometimes difficult to detect a Scaly-finger when it is sitting on the bark of a tree.

BIOLOGY, CARE, AND BREEDING: The interesting thing about this species is its parthenogenesis (females capable of producing young without male fertilization) and related behavior.

The females are very territorial and will scold, chase, and bite encroachers. However, these actions are not performed as intensively as by the males of other gecko species, and vanquished females have not

Muller's Velvet Gecko, *Homopholis mulleri*, is a poorly known species restricted to the Transvaal in southern Africa. Photo by K. H. Switak.

A more widely distributed and common velvet gecko is Wahlberg's Velvet Gecko, *Homopholis wahlbergii*, which ranges over much of southern Africa. It is a large (18 cm), active species that does well in captivity. Photo by K. H. Switak.

been observed to be psychologically affected.

The care of this species is as described for *Heteronotia binoei*. The diet is not difficult, as it will take the usual insects providing they are the right size. It also has a sweet tooth and has been known to lap up jam, sweetened tea and coffee, as well as the nectar from flowers. The provision of calcium and vitamin supplements is essential to keep it in good health. Otherwise softening of the bones will occur and the eggs will not be adequately shelled. Females will devour any soft-shelled eggs they lay and will also eat the shells of those that have already hatched.

With an adequate diet, female Scaly-fingers are very productive, laying one or two eggs every 14-60 days. The eggs are affixed to bark, leaf axils, or the terrarium wall. The slightly oval eggs are about 5 mm in diameter. The 35-37 mm young hatch in 68-93 days. The best results occur if the eggs are left where they are laid (sometimes there is no alternative) and regular spraying is continued. In good terrarium conditions a hatching rate of 90% is not unusual.

The hatchlings should be separated from the adults and reared on small crickets, wax moth larvae, and fruitflies. They develop very quickly and can be sexually mature in eight months. This robust little gecko can be bred on a regular basis. It has no great demands regarding the terrarium and furnishings, making it ideal for the beginner.

Pachydactylus rugosus, an unusual South African member of a large and complex genus. Photo by Paul Freed.

Bibron's Gecko, *Pachydactylus bibroni*, a large species that makes a satisfactory pet when it can be obtained. Photo by Kenneth T. Nemuras.

Pachydactylus marinquensis from southwestern Africa. Photo by Paul Freed.

Above: An adult *Pachydactylus weberi*, a species from the deserts of southwestern Africa. Below is a juvenile of a *Pachydactylus* species, possibly *P. weberi*, but not certainly identifiable. Photos by Paul Freed.

Lygodactylus picturatus
Painted Dwarf Gecko

RANGE: East Africa from Ethiopia in the north to Mozambique in the south. Inland to northern Zimbabwe, Zambia, and eastern Zaire. It also occurs on the islands of Mafia and Zanzibar off the coast of Tanzania.

DESCRIPTION: This diurnal species reaches a total length of 86 mm and has a remarkable sexual dimorphism. The head and shoulders of the male are bright yellow with a pattern of dark brown spots and stripes. The body, limbs, and tail are bluish gray. The throat is black and the belly yellow. The female is more somberly colored, either plain brown or with a sprinkling of light and dark flecks. Her belly is white, and the throat may be whitish or marbled in light and dark colors. Males are territorial, and those that are vanquished by more dominant specimens take on the color of the females. Juveniles are also colored similarly to the adult females.

The most significant characteristic of this species is the round pupil, which indicates that it is diurnal. It is also remarkable in having two rows of adhesive lamellae on the underside of the tail tip. The inner toe is, as in *Phelsuma*

Lygodactylus bradfieldi, a dwarf (6 cm) gecko from the arid savannahs of Namibia. Photo by Paul Freed.

species, only rudimentary. The other toes are widened to the tip and furnished with adhesive pads. There are small claws on the toe-tips. Males possess 6-12 pre-anal pores.

BIOLOGY, CARE, AND BREEDING: This species spends most of its time on the trunks of large trees, usually at a height of 1-2 m. When threatened, it will flee to the other side of the trunk and then ascend higher into the tree. It has been observed that in the breeding season only one pair inhabits each tree trunk. The male courts the female by taking on bright colors, expanding his black throat pouch, and making nodding movements and standing sideward to her. This behavior is also used as a territorial threat to other males. As the males are so aggressive, it is best to keep only one pair per terrarium.

A small terrarium, 30 x 30 x 40 cm, is adequate for a pair of these geckos. The substrate can consist of a potting compost/ sand mixture. A strong, twiggy branch or tree root can be provided for climbing and basking in natural sunlight or under a heat lamp. This species requires strong light, including ultraviolet rays, so a daylight fluorescent tube or a quartz-halogen lamp should be installed (the lamp should be fixed at a sufficient height above the container to avoid overheating). Climbing plants such as *Scindapsus aureus* (pothos) should be arranged away from the direct rays of the lamp. The

daytime temperature should be in the region of 25-32°C, reduced to 18-22°C at night. The interior should be lightly sprayed every day. As well as the usual foods, these geckos can occasionally be given a piece of mashed ripe banana.

The female lays two hard-shelled eggs (5 x 3 mm) that usually adhere to each other. The piece of bark or twig on which the eggs are laid should be removed to an incubator. Incubation time depends on the temperature; at 28–30°C the young will hatch in 45 days, but at lower temperatures (daytime 22–25°C, night 19°C) it will take around 78 days. Incubation periods of even 95 days are known. During incubation the relative air humidity should be maintained around 80%. The hatchlings are best reared in a small container (sandwich box or margarine container) with a gauze lid. A little sand or a piece of foam rubber and a piece of bark are all that is required for furnishings. They may be fed on fruitflies, small wax moth larvae, and newly hatched crickets. Provision of calcium and vitamins, as well as a quota of ultraviolet light, is important to prevent nutritional disorders. It is advisable to give the young geckos five minutes under an ultraviolet lamp two or three times per week.

The young will become sexually mature in less than one year.

Lygodactylus picturatus is a small, very attractive gecko

which demands particular care. It is therefore recommended for more experienced herpetologists.

Paroedura pictus
Madagascar Leaf-toed Gecko

RANGE: Western, southern, and eastern Madagascar.

HABITAT: Savannah and semi-desert areas. Unlike many other Madagascan geckos, it is not dependent on forests.

DESCRIPTION: The most prominent feature of this terrestrial gecko is its large head perched on a short, cylindrical body. Its slender limbs give it an unexpected agility.

The body is covered with small scales plus a few rows of larger keeled scales. Large spine-like scales are present on the tail. The adhesive toe-pads are similar to those in *Phyllodactylus*, and *Paroedura pictus* was originally included in that genus. A small leaf-like pad occurs at the tip of each toe on either side of the claw. Only young specimens up to a few weeks old have any climbing ability on smooth surfaces (such as glass) with these weak pads.

The ground color of the adults is a deep chocolate brown with white and cream spots. Traces of the juvenile pattern (four or five dark-bordered light yellow transverse bands on a light brown background) may be made out with difficulty.

BIOLOGY, CARE, AND BREEDING: This species is best kept in a medium sized terrarium (28–32°C daytime, 22–25°C night temperatures) with a potting compost/sand mixture as substrate and cork bark or

The Festive Gecko, *Narudasia festiva*, a tiny species (under 6 cm) that is active during the day in its Namibian homelands. Photo by Paul Freed.

stones as hiding places. With daily spraying this substrate is ideal in that the lower layers will remain slightly moist. By warming part of the substrate, the females will then be provided with an ideal egg-laying site. Under these conditions the eggs can remain in the terrarium for incubation. The adults will not attack the young (head/body length 26–28 mm, tail 20–24 mm; weight averaging 0.47 g), which hatch in approximately two months. They may then be removed for separate rearing. Of course, the eggs also can be artificially incubated. With a temperature range of 26–29°C and a relative air humidity of 60–70%, the young will hatch in 54–64 days.

The young are easy to rear on small crickets and wax moth larvae. It has been observed that growing specimens can develop a fatty liver. It is therefore advisable to give adequate roughage in the form of crickets and to give wax moth larvae only sparingly. They grow very quickly.

Sex distinction is easy in this species. The male has a

Phelsuma cepediana, the Blue-tailed Day Gecko of Mauritius, is one of the more commonly seen species. The large red spots and bluish tail are distinctive. Photo by Kenneth T. Nemuras.

The endangered Round Island Day Gecko, *Phelsuma guentheri*, a somber species from a small mascarene island that has been almost denuded of vegetation. Photo by R. G. Sprackland.

relatively larger head, a more robust body, and a swollen tail-base.

Pairing takes place in the early hours of the night. During copulation, the male bites the female's neck. A single fertilization seems to be adequate for several clutches. A female in good condition can lay two or three clutches at intervals of only 14 days. The two eggs are buried in the substrate. Occasionally the second egg is laid on the night following the first.

By maintaining a constant temperature and light cycle throughout the year, this species will remain in breeding condition. The female can go through several breeding cycles per year and become an "egg-producing machine." It has happened that females have "laid themselves to death." This can be prevented by separating the sexes after two or three clutches and allowing the female to build up her strength again. A good diet (especially *Gryllus bimaculatus*) and vitamin/mineral supplements are essential.

Paroedura pictus can be regarded as an easy-to-keep species that with adequate care and diet will breed all the year around.

Phelsuma madagascariensis grandis
Giant Madagascar Day Gecko

RANGE: Extreme northern Madagascar.

HABITAT: In trees and on walls of banana plantations and native houses.

DESCRIPTION: Apart from *P. standingi*, *P. m. grandis*, with a total length of 280 mm, is the largest Madagascar day gecko.

The color is light green with a scarlet pattern. A narrow stripe runs from the nostril to the eye. On the forehead is a V-shaped mark that can sometimes merge into a triangle. There are three spots behind the eye. On the lower back, the red spots have a tendency to form bands. There are some specimens without the back spots or even the V-shaped head marking, but all members of this subspecies have the snout stripe. The back pattern can also be different in juveniles and can change continually through the reptile's life.

BIOLOGY, CARE, AND BREEDING: A terrarium with minimum dimensions of 50 x 40 x 60 cm is required for a pair of these large geckos. Furnishings include

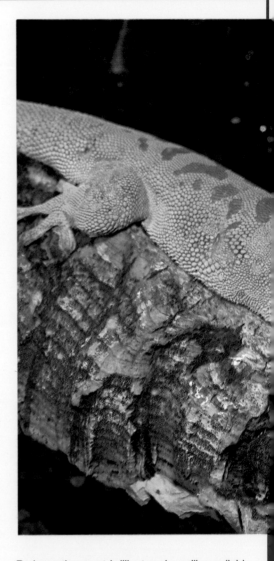

Perhaps the most brilliant and readily available day gecko is *Phelsuma madagascariensis grandis*, the Giant Madagascar Day Gecko. Its large size (28 cm), bright green color, red head pattern, and adaptability make this one of the best pet geckos, though they may be expensive. Photo above by R. D. Bartlett, that at right by H. Zimmermann.

strong branches and tubes of cork bark. Potted plants such as *Sanseveria* and *Scindapsus* can be set into a substrate of potting compost and sand that is warmed with a heat cable. The

lumps in special cups. Remember that honey or sugar water is also often recommended.

Adequate lighting is very important for *Phelsuma* species if they are to live long and reproduce successfully. Apart from the standard daylight fluorescent tubes, the reptiles should be given a daily quota (5–10 minutes) of ultraviolet light from a special UV lamp. Light duration should be 13–14 hours per day in the summer, 10–11 hours in the winter. The temperature should be kept around 30°C during the day, reduced to 20–22°C at night. A relative air humidity of 50–60% is adequate.

The female lays two hard-shelled eggs, sometimes only one

female will like to use the plant pots as egg-laying sites, or the eggs may be laid in the cork bark. *Phelsuma* species do not like to descend to the substrate, so the drinking vessel should be affixed to a branch or to the decorated back wall of the terrarium. A bird drinking fountain could also be used. Drinking water should always contain a vitamin supplement.

Many authors recommend extra calcium for all *Phelsuma* species, often supplied as edible

A day in the life of *Phelsuma madagascariensis*. Photos by Rolf Heselhaus.

Left: Using the large, flexible tongue to lick calcium powder from a leaf. Day geckos require tremendous amounts of calcium for best health.

Right: Displaying in the light.

Below: Lunch break.

Above: Defending territory from an intruder.

The round pupil and broad toes typical of *Phelsuma* are shown by this *Phelsuma madagascariensis*. Virtually all *Phelsuma* have at least some green in the color pattern, although adults may replace the green with other (often equally as bright) colors. Photo by Burkhard Kahl.

The amount of red on the body of *Phelsuma madagascariensis* varies from individual to individual and within different populations and subspecies. Some lack all red and have a reduced red bridle as well. Photo at left by H. Hansen, that below by William B. Allen, Jr.

Above: A nearly all-green *Phelsuma madagascariensis*. Below: The green Madagascar Day Gecko, *Phelsuma madagascariensis kochi*. Photo by Kenneth T. Nemuras.

Top: A brightly patterned young *Phelsuma madagascariensis*. Photo by Rolf Heselhaus. Below: *Phelsuma cepediana* from Mauritius. Photo by Kenneth T. Nemuras.

in rare cases. They are deposited in a dark corner or simply on the surface of the earth in a plant pot. During the breeding season (March to July in the terrarium) up to six clutches may be produced at intervals of two to six weeks. At an incubation temperature of around 28°C and 65–75% relative humidity, the 65–70 mm juveniles will hatch in an average of 64 days. They should be reared with all of the optimum conditions recommended for the adults.

Phelsuma laticauda
Flat-tailed Day Gecko, Gold-Dust Day Gecko

RANGE: Northwestern Madagascar, the island of Nossi

Phelsuma laticauda, the Gold-dust Day Gecko or Flat-tailed Day Gecko. Actually, the tail is not nearly as flat as in several other species, but the name "gold-dust" seems very descriptive of the pattern. Adults often become more golden and less green with maturity. Photo at right by Burkhard Kahl, that below by Kenneth T. Nemuras.

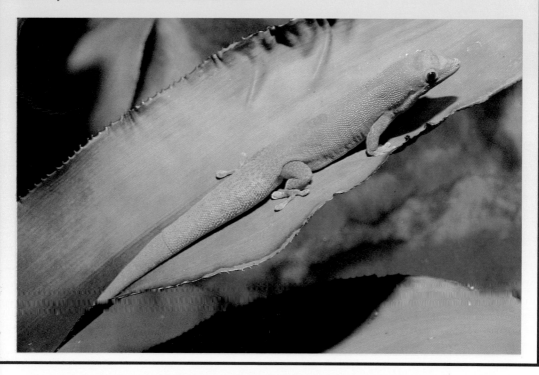

Be, and Anjouan and Mayotte, in the Comoros.

HABITAT: Found mainly on banana trees but in some areas also on the walls of houses.

DESCRIPTION: This species is undoubtedly one of the most attractive members of the genus *Phelsuma*. The ground color is yellowish green. There are two red bands running over the snout. The forepart of the back is set with golden yellow scales. At the rear of the back are three regular red patches followed by smaller red spots toward the tail. A characteristic of the species is the sky blue eye-ring. With a total length of 120 mm (head/body 58 mm, tail 60 mm), *P. laticauda* is one of the smaller members of the genus.

BIOLOGY, CARE, AND BREEDING: A terrarium with minimum dimensions of 40 x 20 x 30 cm is suitable for a pair of these geckos. It is best to keep them in individual pairs as with most *Phelsuma* species. Fairly robust climbing twigs are essential, and one or two bromeliad plants will not go amiss. The female will lay her eggs in the leaf bracts of these plants. A bird drinking fountain and a little dish to contain honey water or mashed banana should be provided. If vitaminized water is always available, spraying will be unneccessary.

The temperature of the terrarium should be maintained between 24 and 28°C during the day but reduced to 18–20°C at night. This species can tolerate temperatures as low as 15°C for short periods.

They may be fed with the usual food insects every two or three days. Be sure that enough roughage is provided by supplying a good variety of food items. Also, they must have the possibility of ingesting tiny stones (to 1 mm in diameter).

The female lays two (occasionally one) hard-shelled eggs. Six clutches at intervals of three to eight weeks may be laid per breeding season. They are usually laid in the narrow leaf axils of bromeliads or *Sanseveria* (if provided) and occasionally under bark on the substrate. After three or four clutches there is usually a rest period. During this time you can help by reducing the food and holding the temperature at 20°C for two or three months. After this, return to the normal regime of temperature and feeding.

The eggs are most successfully incubated at temperatures between 25 and 28° C and a relative air humidity of 60–80%. At a constant temperature of 28°C, the young will hatch in 40 days; if the temperature fluctuates between the figures given above, it will take up to 63 days.

The hatchlings may be reared on fruitflies, newly hatched crickets, and the smallest of wax moth larvae. The food items should be dusted with a calcium preparation and the drinking water should be mineralized; regular ultraviolet light is important for problem-free rearing.

The Gold-dust Day Gecko, *Phelsuma laticauda*. Notice the rather intricate pattern of the head, with the blue spot on the upper eyelid. Blue spots at various positions on the head and shoulders are found in several day geckos and probably aid in species identification in the wild. Photos by Kenneth T. Nemuras.

Above: A side view of *Phelsuma cepediana* shows the contrast of red, green, and brown on the flanks typical of the species. Photo by G. Marcuse. Below: *Phelsuma astriata*, a seldom seen species from the Seychelles. Photo by Kenneth T. Nemuras.

A portrait of the Blue-tailed Day Gecko, *Phelsuma cepediana*, showing the intricate brilliance of its pattern and the pebble-like texture of the scales. This specimen has more blue on the back than most. Notice the large blue spot on the snout. Photo by J. Visser.

On these two pages are shown specimens of the Peacock Day Gecko, *Phelsuma quad-riocellata*. This Madagascan species is instantly recognizable by the round black spot behind each front leg. The spots are encircled by a narrow blue ring, often not conspicuous. Although red spots and scribbling are present on the back and may be quite numerous in some specimens, the red is never conspicuous. The blue on the snout is diffuse and does not form a distinct, strongly outlined spot as in some other species. Photos by Kenneth T. Nemuras.

The Seychelles Giant Day Gecko, *Phelsuma sundbergi*. The genus *Phelsuma* is virtually restricted to the Seychelles, Madagascar, the Mascarenes, and adjacent islands in the western Indian Ocean. Most species in the hobby come from Madagascar. Photo by Kenneth T. Nemuras.

Above right and facing page: One of the more delicately patterned day geckos is the Striped Day Gecko, *Phelsuma lineata*, of Madagascar. The juvenile above shows relatively more red on the back than the adult at the right, but the distinctive reddish stripe over a white lower side remains the same regardless of age. This species has been confused with *Phelsuma cepediana*, which has large red spots on the back and brownish lower sides beneath a green stripe. Photos by Paul Freed.

As more and more species are bred in captivity and keepers determine exact requirements for each species, day geckos should become more readily available at lower prices. Just remember that day geckos require large amounts of calcium, most easily administered in the form of ground cuttlebone mixed with an equal amount of reptile or bird vitamins. Photo by Burkhard Kahl.

Until recently, *Phelsuma standingi*, the Banded Day Gecko of southern Madagascar was known from only a few specimens. With continuing deforestation of the region, more and more Madagascan reptiles have reached the market, and some, such as the Banded Day Gecko, have become moderately common in captivity. Photo by Kenneth T. Nemuras.

Phelsuma dubia
Bright-eyed Day Gecko

RANGE: This species has one of the greatest ranges in the genus, reaching from northwestern Madagascar through the Comoros (Anjouan, Great Comoro, Mayotte, Moheli) to the coastal areas of East Africa (the island of Zanzibar and coastal Tanzania).

HABITAT: The large range indicates that it is adaptable to varied habitats. It may be found in banana trees, in other vegetation, and on walls.

DESCRIPTION: This medium sized *Phelsuma* (male to 153 mm, female to 160 mm) is very variable in color, ranging from greenish blue through leaf green to various shades of gray (blue-gray, olive-gray, gray-brown). Brown flecks are situated on the rear portion of the back. A characteristic that helps distinguish this species from other *Phelsuma* species is the orange to yellow iris.

BIOLOGY, CARE, AND BREEDING: The terrarium and furnishings are as described for the preceding species. Temperature and humidity are also similar, but one should opt for stronger lighting so that these geckos can show their colors at their best.

This species is easy to breed in the terrarium; a female can lay up to ten clutches of two eggs per year. The eggs adhere to bark or the terrarium wall. With an incubation temperature of 25–28°C and a relative humidity of 65–75%, the young will hatch in 40–50 days. The juveniles are about 45.8 mm in length and slightly different in color from the adults. The ground color is gray-brown with a bronze shimmer. Irregular light green patches decorate the back. In 9–12 months they will grow to adult size and take on the adult colors. This species is highly recommended for the beginner.

Phyllodactylus europaeus
European Leaf-toed Gecko

RANGE: This species inhabits islands in the western Mediterranean such as the Iles d' Hyeres of the southern coast of France, Elba, Capri, Palmajola, Pianosa, Montecristo, Corsica, and Sardinia. It is also found on the islands of Galitone, Aguglia, and Cani off the coast of Tunis. It is found on the mainland only near the towns of Genoa, La Spezia, and Lerici, and near Monte Argentario in Italy.

HABITAT: The habitat of *P. europaeus* is as varied as the islands on which they live. While it may be found under stones on one island, it may live under loose bark or in ground litter on another. Rock crevices and spaces between boulders are further favored habitats. It is rarely found on buildings.

DESCRIPTION: With a total length of 80 mm, *P. europaeus* is the smallest European gecko. The majority of specimens actually reach a length of only 60–70 mm.

The head is egg-shaped and well set off from the slightly flattened body. A narrow fold of

Above: *Phelsuma sundbergi*, the Seychelles Giant Day Gecko. Photo by R. G. Sprackland. Below: Portrait of the Banded Day Gecko, *Phelsuma standingi*. Photo by Kenneth T. Nemuras.

Above: Portrait of *Phelsuma sundbergi*. Notice the blue area on the lips. Photo by Kenneth T. Nemuras. Below: *Phyllodactylus lineatus* of southern Africa. Photo by Paul Freed.

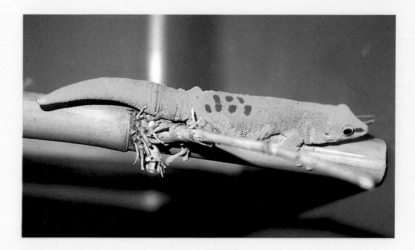

The keeper of geckos as pets will never be lacking in variety. Few lizard families can boast of such variation in colors and habitat requirements as the geckos. Consider the two extremes shown here. Above is a typical Madagascar Day Gecko, *Phelsuma madagascariensis*, a species requiring high humidities and temperatures, lots of calcium in the diet, a planted terrarium, and active during the day. Its bright colors attract attention anywhere. Below is *Phyllodactylus xanti*, a leaf-toed gecko from arid western Mexico north to southern California. It is nocturnal in habits, found in minimally vegetated dry savannahs and deserts, very dull in pattern, unassuming in diet and behavior, and likely to escape notice in almost any terrarium. Photo above by Elaine Radford, that below by Robert S. Simmons.

skin runs along the flanks. The round tail is strong and begins to taper only in the middle. The male has relatively large tubercular scales on either side of the tail base. In the female the tail can be constricted at the base, forming a sort of turnip shape. Regenerated tails in both sexes take on this shape and are relatively shorter. The tail is also somewhat prehensile. The limbs are relatively short. Each toe is furnished with a single claw and a pair of leaf-like adhesive pads at its tip.

The body is covered with small, flat scales; it is the only European species without tubercular scales on the back. The males are blackish in color with tiny silver-gray spots and flecks sometimes arranged in a reticulate pattern. The females are usually plain gray with only a weak pattern.

BIOLOGY, CARE, AND BREEDING: This species is active mainly at dusk, but occasionally it basks in the late afternoon or early morning sun. It moves with a deliberate and elegant gait, but if alarmed it can show a surprising turn of agility as it retreats to a refuge. It stalks its prey and pounces in the manner of a cat. In the wild it feeds on ants, woodlice, mosquitos, and small moths. In the terrarium it can be fed on wax moth larvae, crickets, and flies (*Drosophila*, houseflies, etc.).

The European Leaf-toed Gecko requires husbandry similar to that described for *Alsophylax laevis*. As with other European gecko species, our knowledge of its reproductive behavior is inadequate. In the wild the females are thought to lay their almost spherical eggs (8 x 9 mm) in June in rock crevices. In most cases there are two eggs per clutch, but occasionally only one.

At an incubation temperature of 25–28°C and a relative humidity of 50–60%, the young have hatched in 65–118 days in captivity. They may be reared on the smallest wax moth larvae, crickets, aphids, and fruitflies. They grow very quickly but take three years to reach sexual maturity.

This is a long-lived species that has been kept alive for 20 years in the terrarium. Due to its current legal protection in most of its range, it is hoped that future terrarium stocks will be maintained by breeding those that are already held in captivity.

Ptychozoon lionatum
Fringed Gecko, Flying Gecko

RANGE: Southern Burma, Thailand, and the island of Ramri.

HABITAT: The original habitat of this species is deep in the rain forest, but it seems to be quite adaptable and is now frequently found around human habitations.

DESCRIPTION: The head, body, and tail are flattened and covered with small scales. There are no large tubercular scales on the back. Characteristic of the genus are the webbed toes and

Ptychozoon lionatum, the common Fringed Gecko or Flying Gecko. Photo by Kenneth T. Nemuras.

the flap of loose skin extending from the sides of the head along the flanks and tail.

In contrast to the gliding agamid lizards (*Draco*, the flying dragons) found in the same habitat, the skin flaps of these geckos are not strengthened with elongated ribs or particularly well developed muscles, so they cannot be voluntarily opened. However, the skin flaps will open when the geckos are leaping from limb to limb and act in much the same way as a parachute, allowing the reptiles to glide and drop relatively greater distances than other species. When the gecko is at rest the skin flaps fold along the flanks and are barely discernible. The tail flaps are scalloped but are smooth toward the tip. The toes are clawed and furnished with well-developed adhesive pads.

P. lionatum grows to a little more than 160 mm, of which approximately half is taken up by the tail. The color is a uniform gray-brown with four wavy transverse bands across the back. A further six bands are arranged along the tail.

BIOLOGY, CARE, AND BREEDING: As its habitat suggests, this species requires a humid terrarium. Planting is not strictly necessary, as the reptiles normally spend their time on the bark and branches of trees. Plants can, however, be used to create a pleasing effect in the terrarium. Substrate may consist of a peat/sand mixture. A few pieces of cork bark,

branches, and twigs will complete the furnishings. In addition to regular spraying, a water dish is essential.

For a breeding group of four or five geckos, a terrarium should have a minimum size of 60 x 40 x 80 cm. The daytime temperature should be maintained between 28 and 32°C but may be reduced by 5–6°C at night. A daytime humidity of 50–60% and a nighttime humidity of 100% can be maintained through regular spraying.

P. lionatum is very productive, and females can lay eggs all through the year if given the right conditions. Usually two (sometimes one) eggs (11–14 mm) per clutch are affixed to bark or stones. The female will return time and again to the same egg-laying site.

The 55 mm young will hatch in 68–75 days at an incubation temperature of 25–28°C and a relative humidity of 65–80%. Although the adults rarely attack their offspring, it is best to rear them in separate accommodations. It is interesting to note that the adults will eat the egg shells after the young have hatched.

The juvenile diet consists of the usual gecko food. Depending on the quantity and variety given, the young will be fully grown in one to two years, at which time they are usually already sexually mature. Males possess 16–28 prominent pre-anal pores and a flap of skin on either side of the cloaca. These

Flying Geckos have long been popular with hobbyists, but only recently have they become available in reasonable quantities. They are not difficult to keep and breed, and they are so bizarre they are sure to attract attention. Photo by L. Edmonds.

Underview of *Ptychozoon lionatum*. Notice the lateral skin fold in a relaxed position held close to the side of the body. The broad webs between the toes are especially conspicuous here. Photo by Kenneth T. Nemuras.

When at rest, most of the parachute membranes of the Flying Gecko are not readily visible, only the fringes on the tail being constantly erect. This rather large gecko has become moderately common on the market now and makes a good pet. Photo by Kenneth T. Nemuras.

are absent in the female.

RELATED SPECIES: *Ptychozoon kuhli* grows a little larger than *P. lionatum*, reaching a total length of 190 mm, and has dorsal tubercles. It requires similar husbandry. *P. kuhli* also is readily bred in the terrarium. The young will hatch from the two hard-shelled eggs in 90 days if incubated at a temperature of 24–26°C.

Ptyodactylus hasselquistii Fan-fingered Gecko

RANGE: This species occurs in a wide range from the Atlas Mountains of Morocco in the west to the Gulf of Aden in the east, and from the Mediterranean coast to the southern edge of the Sahara (Mali, northern Togo, northern Nigeria, Chad, and Sudan). In addition, it has colonized the Arabian Peninsula (Israel, Lebanon, Syria, Jordan, Saudi Arabia, Iraq, and Iran), as well as several islands in the Arabian Sea.

HABITAT: The Fan-finger is vertically oriented and is found on cliff faces, stone walls, house walls, and in ravines. It is rarely found on trees or wooden houses. In mountainous areas it occurs to an altitude of 1800 m.

DESCRIPTION: At first glance this species gives one the impression that it is poorly nourished. It has

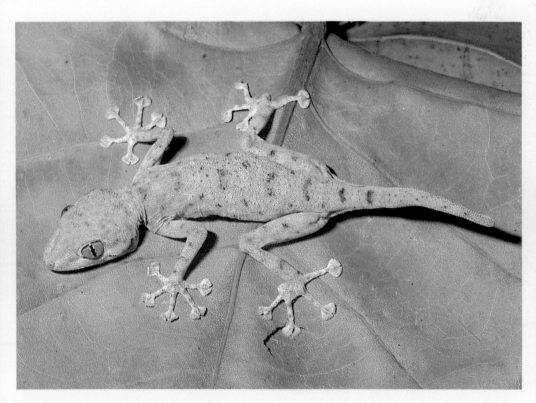

Ptyodactylus hasselquistii, the Fan-fingered Gecko, is found over much of northern Africa and the Middle East. Photo above by R. D. Bartlett, that below by E. Zimmermann.

a large head mounted on a long, slender body carried by long, thin limbs. A skin-fold along its flanks furthers the impression of starvation. The fan-shaped adhesive pads on each toe give this species its common name. These pads are so efficient that even dead specimens will cling to the hand or other surfaces.

The ground color is extremely variable—to date, dark green, olive, brown, yellowish, orangish, black, and even whitish individuals have been described. Whitish spots are arranged in the ground color of the back. In some cases these give the impression of dark and light transverse bands.

BIOLOGY, CARE, AND. BREEDING: The Fan-finger is active both during the day and at night. Although it hunts for its prey mainly at dusk and dawn, it will often bask in the sun during the day. Even in the midday heat it may be found in shady spots.

In the higher altitudes of its range it will hibernate for two or three months. In the terrarium, a two to four weeks winter "rest period" will bc adequate, although this is not essential as

A one-day-old *Rhacodactylus chahoua*, a New Caledonian gecko. These are arboreal (tree-climbing) lizards with prehensile tails and an adhesive pad under the tip of the tail for extra security. Brown juveniles often become greenish adults. Unlike most other geckos, *Rhacodactylus* species tend to eat a great amount of fruit. Photo by Paul Freed.

this species relies more on the temperature than on a physiological rhythm.

Little is known about its reproductive behavior. Pairing probably takes place in the spring shortly after hibernation. In Israel, the females start egg-laying in May, continuing until August. During this period three to five clutches of two eggs are laid. At first the eggs are soft-shelled. They are put in cracks and crevices in rocks or under stones, where they adhere to the laying surface.

The eggs, which are almost spherical and average 13–15 mm in diameter, take 90–100 days to hatch in the terrarium. In the wild the young hatch in about two months. The hatchlings are 50 mm in length (head/body 28 mm, tail 22 mm). The young can be reared in the same terrarium as the parents, providing sufficient food is available. Even in the wild, pairs of this species are often found living together with their offspring. In 18–24 months they are fully grown, at about 10 cm in length.

A wall terrarium with a narrow base (60 x 30 cm is adequate) is ideal for this species. The height of the container is more important and should be at least 60 cm. The back wall should be built up with rocks containing controllable hiding places. Pieces of cork bark may also be used. Planting is not strictly necessary, but a shallow vessel of drinking water is essential. As the Fan-finger is very territorial, only a single pair should be kept in each container. Kept at a temperature of around 30°C (locally to 35°C), reduced to 20°C at night, and given a varied diet (moths are eagerly taken), the Fan-finger is a very interesting and long-lived terrarium subject.

Saurodactylus mauritanicus Lizard-fingered Gecko

RANGE: Morocco, North Africa.

HABITAT: This highly recommended terrarium species is found from the coast into the lower foothills of the Atlas Mountains. The nominate form, *S. m. mauritanicus*, is found in the coastal areas, while *S. m. brosseti* occurs more inland. Lizard-fingers inhabit sparsely vegetated, stony country as well as brushland. They hide under rocks during the day, coming out at dusk to hunt for food.

DESCRIPTION: With a total length (head/body 33 mm, tail 27 mm) of 60 mm, this species is one of the smallest geckos. Because they are easy to keep and have an attractive coloration, they are popular terrarium subjects. *S. m. mauritanicus* males have a light to dark brown ground color, while in *S. m. brosseti* the dark brown is broken by numerous golden yellow patches. In both subspecies a yellow stripe stretches from the snout through the eye to the back of the head. The tail is also yellow, marked with brown and black patches. The females of both races are more somberly colored. The body is covered with granular scales. The small toes of this terrestrial species are not furnished with adhesive pads.

BIOLOGY, CARE, AND BREEDING: A small terrarium with dimensions of 30 x 20 x 20 cm is ideal for keeping and breeding this species. A sandy substrate, two or three flat stones arranged on top of each other (but secure), and a shallow drinking vessel will complete the furnishings. An ordinary tungsten bulb can be turned off and the temperature can drop. In the evening the interior of the terrarium should be lightly sprayed to increase the night humidity.

Eventually this species will become active by day in the terrarium and will bask under the lamp or even go hunting for food. As soon as it spots moving food, it will wriggle its round tail horizontally back and forth while creeping slowly toward the prey until it grabs it with lightning speed. It will eat small insects and spiders.

With a little skill, this species can be bred in captivity. The females bury their eggs in a burrow 1 cm deep in the sand. During the laying period (*S. m. mauritanicus* April–August, *S. m. brosseti* May–September) they lay up to eight eggs. The eggs are spherical, very hard-shelled, and about 5 mm in diameter. The 18–22 mm young hatch in 45–60

Saurodactylus mauritanicus, the Lizard-fingered Gecko. Photo by K. H. Switak.

The Australian Beaked Gecko, *Rhynchoedura ornata*. There are several fine-scaled or velvety geckos from Australia that are similar to *Oedura* species in general appearance. Photo by K. H. Switak.

days, depending on the incubation temperature, which should be in the region of 28–30°C.

The hatchlings are plain dark brown to blue-black, and the back pattern of the adults can be vaguely made out. The tail is bright yellow to orange. They may be reared on *Drosophila*, very small crickets, and wax moth larvae.

Tarentola mauritanica
Wall Gecko, Moorish Gecko

RANGE: Iberian Peninsula with the exception of the northwest, the Balearic and Pityusen Islands, southern France, Corsica, Sardinia, many Tyrrhenian islands (Elba, Montecristo), the Italian coast through Sicily, the northern Adriatic and Jugoslavia between Zadar and Dubrovnik, the islands of Ugljan and Hvar, the Ionian Islands (Ithaka, Kephallenia, Zakynthos), Crete, and North Africa from Egypt to the Atlantic in the west.

HABITAT: Found mainly in buildings and ruins, bridges, stone walls, etc. In southern France it may be found in rocky outcrops or stone piles well away from human habitation.

DESCRIPTION: This is a robustly built species that reaches a total length of 160 mm.

The head, body, and ringed tail are distinctly flattened. The large head is prominently set off from the body. A flap of skin runs along the flanks, and the limbs are relatively short. The undersides of the toes are furnished with adhesive pads along their whole length, and the third and fourth toes have large claws. In the female the other toes have small retractile claws.

The body is covered with small angular scales and larger keeled tubercular scales that form 10–16 rows along the back. The ground color of the back varies from the whitish to yellowish brown, dark brown, or almost black. The pattern consists of darker irregular transverse bands that fade as the animal ages. During the day these geckos are darker in color than at night.

BIOLOGY, CARE, AND BREEDING: In spite of its plump appearance, the Wall Gecko is an agile

The Wall Gecko or Moorish Gecko, *Tarentola mauritanica*, of southern Europe and northern Africa. This specimen clearly shows the ringed, rather alligator-like appearance of the tubercles in adults. Photo by K. H. Switak.

In this Wall Gecko the scales are less developed and the gecko looks more like a spiny version of Bibron's Gecko. With growth the pattern will weaken and the scales will become more spiny. Photo by John Coborn.

climber that can run up rock faces and even walk on ceilings and glass windows thanks to its well developed adhesive toe-pads. Although the main activity time is at dusk and during the night, this species may often be seen (depending on the season) sunning itself during the day. The diet of this extremely predatory species is very variable and ranges from various insects and spiders to small lizards.

Although the Wall Gecko has been kept in the terrarium for many years, we do not know a lot about its reproductive behavior. Pairing is similar to that of lacertid (typical) lizards. From the end of April to mid-July the female lays several clutches of two hard-shelled eggs (11 x 14 mm). The eggs are buried or affixed to surfaces in crevices, etc.

There is no sexual color dimorphism, and distinguishing the sexes can be difficult. The males are relatively more strongly built and have a wider head; in addition, they have spine-like scales at the tail-base. The extra small claws on the toes of the females can only help to distinguish the sex in dead animals. Males are extremely territorial, and only a single pair should be kept in a terrarium.

Eggs are best left at the laying site for incubation in a dry substrate (sand, dry leaf litter); they will not tolerate damp conditions. At incubation temperatures of 26–30°C, the young will hatch in 5–12 weeks (depending on whether the temperature is allowed to drop at night).

The about 50 mm hatchlings are more strongly marked than the adults and, in addition, have prominent white spots. In contrast to most other gecko species, the juvenile Wall Geckos take four to five years to reach maturity and are relatively long-lived. During growth the young geckos must be well fed and the food insects should be dusted with a mineral supplement, otherwise nutritional disorders such as rickets will occur.

The care of this species is as described for the Fan-fingered Gecko. In order to increase the likelihood of breeding success, they should be allowed a period of hibernation at reduced temperature and lighting in the winter. This species is highly

Above: The wall gecko of the Canary and Cape Verde Islands is *Tarentola delalandii*, a species not often seen in the hobby. Photo by Horst Bielfeld.

Facing page: This striking gecko is a juvenile *Pachydactylus* from Namibia. With growth the contrasting colors will weaken and only the pale collar will remain somewhat distinct. It is difficult to identify juvenile geckos when they deviate so greatly from the adults. Photo by Paul Freed.

recommended for the beginner. Because of its slow attainment of maturity, only captive-bred specimens should be purchased.

Teratoscincus scincus
Wonder Gecko, Frog-eyed Gecko

RANGE: Southern USSR from the eastern coast of the Caspian Sea to western China, Iran, northern and southern Afghanistan, northwestern

Teratoscincus scincus, the Wonder Gecko. Photo by Ken Lucas, Steinhart Aquarium.

Pakistan, and in the coastal regions of the Arabian peninsula from Qatar through the United Arab Emirates.

HABITAT: A crepuscular and nocturnal species that lives in desert and semi-desert areas, where it digs burrows up to 80 cm deep in sand dunes until it reaches the damp layers.

DESCRIPTION: The Wonder Gecko can reach a total length of 17 cm, but most of them stay a little smaller. The most notable features are the massive head, the large round eyes, and the plate-like scales on the body and tail. The head is covered with small scales. The scalation of this species is very thin and delicate, and with rough handling the skin will pull off in patches. Fortunately the scales will regenerate in acclimated specimens provided they receive an adequate diet; otherwise the animal may be lost. It is surprising to find such a delicate skin on an animal that lives in such a harsh desert environment, but it can be explained by the fact that the skin is involved in respiration and gas exchange. The skin barely protects the reptile from desiccation, which is why it spends the hottest parts of the day deep in its relatively damp burrow.

Further adaptations for living in a desert environment include the comb-like "eyelashes" and the comb-like borders of the toes that, respectively, protect the eyes from sand and allow the reptile to move through loose sand.

The coloration is very attractive. The pale to bright yellow ground color is patterned with brown to nearly black flecks and stripes. The belly, which is also covered in fish-like scales, is plain white. The large scales on the dorsal surface of the tail are gray.

BIOLOGY, CARE, and BREEDING: Due to its attractive coloration

Teratoscincus scincus often is called the Frog-eyed Gecko, based on the large eyes in a short, broad head. The broad scales are seldom found in other geckos and are not typical of all members of the genus. These are among the most unusual of the geckos, with very particular environmental requirements. Photo by Burkhard Kahl.

and its interesting habits, the Wonder Gecko, although not always readily available, is a much prized subject for the terrarium. Its natural life style must, of course, be reflected in its captive husbandry. A terrarium with minimum dimensions of 40 x 40 x 40 cm is suitable for a pair. A sand substrate at least 10 cm deep is essential. The lower layer should be kept moist. This can be achieved by sinking a porous earthenware pipe into the substrate and occasionally pouring a small amount of water into it. Such pipes are also good as hiding places because they will hold moisture.

With the use of a heat cable and a heat lamp, the daytime temperature can be raised to 32–35°C (locally to 40°C), but heating appliances must be turned off at night so the temperature falls to 20–22°C. A difference of 10°C in day and night temperatures is extremely important. The burrows should be lightly sprayed every day, and a dish of drinking water should also be available. A two-to-three-week winter rest period at lower temperatures should be allowed so the lizards come into breeding condition.

During the breeding season, the females lay up to four clutches of usually two hard-shelled eggs. These eggs are 17–21 mm long, 16–19 mm wide, and weigh between 2.5 and 3 grams. The eggs are very delicate and must be handled with the greatest of care. They

The Small-scaled Wonder Gecko, *Teratoscincus microlepis*, a more "normal" gecko with environmental requirements similar to its more bizarre cousin. Photo by Robert S. Simmons.

may be laid on the surface of the sand or buried. Gravid females can become extremely aggressive toward the males, which do not defend themselves. As this can lead to fatal skin damage in the males, gravid females are best removed to separate housing.

In contrast to the eggs of many other gecko species, those of the Wonder Gecko require a relatively low humidity to develop. A relative humidity of 40–65% and a temperature of 28–32°C should be provided. The eggs can be placed on a sand surface or kept among clean wood shavings. They can also be left at the laying site, but should be covered with an upturned flowerpot so they are not disturbed by the female in her burrowing activities. This will also prevent the newly hatched young from becoming a meal for the adult.

Under these conditions the young will hatch in 72–93 days. The hatchlings are quite large, 62 mm, and they weigh 1.58–1.89 g. With adequate feeding (small crickets, wax moth larvae, and cockroaches plus vitamin/mineral supplements) the young will reach full size within one year.

In the wild, this species feeds mainly on beetles, but it will thrive on the usual gecko food insects in captivity.

A description of the Wonder Gecko would be incomplete without mention of its threatening behavior. Standing high-legged and wriggling its tail horizontally, it produces chirping noises with its large plate-like scales and presents an imposing sight to an aggressor. Should this not be sufficient to frighten an intruder, it will bark and throw itself into an attack, biting fiercely. Such behavior is only seen in the males; the females are much more peaceful.

In captivity, the behavior is gradually lost.

RELATED SPECIES: *Teratoscincus microlepis,* the Small-scaled Wonder Gecko from southeastern Iran, southern Afghanistan, and northwestern Pakistan, requires similar captive conditions to *T. scincus.* The eggs (19 x 15 mm) will hatch in 46–48 days if given a constant incubation temperature of 35°C and a humidity of 60–70%. All *Teratoscincus* species should be kept only by experienced herpetologists. They are perhaps the most unusual of the geckos.

This little burrowing gecko from Australia, *Nephrurus levis*, the Knob-tailed Gecko, bears many similarities in form to the Small-scaled Wonder Gecko although the two are not especially close relatives. Notice the rows of tubercles on the tail of the Australian species. Photo by K. H. Switak.

Thecadactylus rapicauda
Turnip-tailed Gecko

RANGE: Mexico, Central America, northern South America (from northeastern Brazil westward to Ecuador), and the Caribbean islands of Trinidad, Tobago, Aruba, Curacao, Bonaire, and Los Testigos.

HABITAT: Inhabits trees in rainforest areas, but also may be found in human habitations in forested areas.

DESCRIPTION: The Turnip-tail reaches 220 mm in length (head/body 121 mm, tail 96.8 mm). In contrast to most other gecko species, the male is somewhat smaller than the female and not so robustly built. The body is covered with small granular scales that give the skin a satin-like texture. The flattish head is prominently set off from the body. The body of the female is somewhat less flattened than that of the male. The unregenerated tail is also flat and is used as an extra "limb" or prop for climbing among the foliage. As the tail is

The Turnip-tailed Gecko, *Thecadactylus rapicauda*, of tropical America is not especially distinguished in appearance but makes a fine pet. Photo by Kenneth T. Nemuras.

Most Turnip-tails have regenerated tails that are round in cross-section rather than flattened in the original form. The adhesive lamellae are extremely well-developed in this climbing species. Photo by Kenneth T. Nemuras.

easily lost through autotomy, many adults have a regenerated tail that is no longer as efficient, but some regenerated tails take on the turnip-like appearance that gives the species its common name. The skin also pulls off very easily.

The adhesive pads situated on the undersides of the widened toes consist of two rows of lamellae. These are so well developed that even dead specimens will stick to a smooth vertical surface. With the exception of each of the first toes, all other toes possess a strong 1-mm-long claw. Situated between the two rows of

lamellae, the claws can be retracted as the reptile moves over smooth surfaces.

The ground color varies from light brown through dark brown to light or dark gray with a light green shimmer. The pattern consists of black and white spots and streaks. The lip scales are white with black borders.

BIOLOGY, CARE, AND BREEDING: The Turnip-tail is mainly active at night but may sometimes bask in the sun. Its normal movement is slow and ponderous, but it can show a turn of speed if threatened. If it is cornered it will open its mouth wide and show its blue tongue. If

Detail of the head of the Turnip-tailed Gecko, *Thecadactylus rapicauda*. Notice the extremely fine scalation with few or no enlarged tubercular scales. Even the eyes continue the brownish coloration of the body. Photo by Kenneth T. Nemuras.

this does not help, it will bite fiercely. Otherwise this is a placid species that lives peacefully with other (even smaller) geckos, including its own offspring. Several males can be kept together providing there are no females present.

Information on the reproductive behavior of this species is sparse. My specimens paired at night and in the manner of most other geckos. Gravidity and egg-laying unfortunately could not be observed, so no figures for incubation can be given. Depending on the area, wild female Turnip-tails may be gravid from May to September.

The nearly round eggs (18 x 20 mm) have very hard shells and are buried by the female in a slightly moist substrate. The two young hatch within an interval of 13 days and measure 85 cm in length (head/body 48 mm, tail 37 mm). They are light brown with seven wavy crossbands. Three white bands with a dark border on the front edge run across the tail. The whole of the tail-tip is white.

Although the young are not normally attacked by the adults, they should be reared in separate terraria. Rearing poses no great problems.

Captive care of this species is as described for *Ptychozoon lionatum*, but furnishings and plants should be relatively more robust. Both young and adult Turnip-tails can be fed on the usual food insects, but some individuals will take pinkie mice. The Turnip-tail belongs to the "easy to keep" category. Breeding is possible but not common.

Portrait of a Flat-tailed Gecko, *Uroplatus fimbriatus*. These Madagascan geckos are slow-moving nocturnal lizards that depend on camouflage for safety. Photo by Robert S. Simmons.

A glance at the tail of *Uroplatus fimbriatus* readily reveals the source of both the common name (Flat-tailed Gecko) and the generic name (also flat-tailed). The scales along the lower side are modified to produce a serrated edge that helps the gecko disappear on tree bark as it presses against the trunk, motionless and head-down. Photo by Robert S. Simmons.

Night lizards, family Xanthusiidae, often resemble geckos by having very fine, granular scales. They also often occur in similar tropical American habitats. Unlike geckos, however, they have large head scales arranged much like the scales of more typical lizards. This is *Xanthusia henshawi* of southern California. Photo by K. H. Switak.

SPHERE-FINGERED GECKOS

(SUBFAMILY SPHAERODACTYLINAE)

The subfamily Sphaerodactylinae contains the genera *Coleodactylus, Gonatodes, Lepidoblepharis, Pseudogonatodes,* and *Sphaerodactylus,* all found in the New World between latitudes 26° in the north and 22° in the south. In addition, some species are found on the Cocos and Galapagos Islands of the eastern Pacific as well as many of the Caribbean islands.

All are small diurnal or crepuscular species. The smallest of all geckos are contained in this subfamily, and some of them can compete with the chameleons in the genus *Brookesia* as being the smallest lizards in the world. The males of the Colombian species *Lepidoblepharis sanctaemartae* reach only 40 mm in length; the oval eggs of this species are just 3.5 mm in length.

The colonization of the New World by these geckos probably took place in the early Tertiary, and they are probably descended from the ancestors of today's *Pristurus* species. The success of the subfamily in its colonization of the New World is reflected in over 60 species in just the genus *Sphaerodactylus,* and this in spite of the fact that all sphere-fingers reproduce with just a

The least geckos or reef geckos, genus *Sphaerodactylus,* represent some 60 species of small lizards plus numerous subspecies on various Caribbean islands. Many exhibit different color patterns when young and differences in pattern between sexes. All this makes it almost impossible to correctly identify lizards from photos. This *Sphaerodactylus* from Grand Cayman seems to be *S. notatus,* a species widely distributed in the Caribbean and introduced accidentally to many islands. Photo by Dr. Guido Dingerkus.

single egg per clutch. The identification of sphere-fingered geckos is difficult at best.

Sphaerodactylus cinereus
Ashy Gecko

RANGE: The Caribbean islands of Cuba, Hispaniola, and Navassa. Introduced into the Florida Keys.

HABITAT: During the day, this species hides in wall cavities, among stone piles, and in vegetation. At dusk it goes into houses or onto street lamps in search of food insects.

DESCRIPTION: The Ashy Gecko has a total length of 73 mm, of which 37 mm is taken up by the head and body. The head tapers to a pointed, slightly flattened snout. Like the rest of the body and tail, the head is covered with small granular scales. There is a row of needle-like ciliary scales ("eyelashes") across the top of the eye. The thin toes each are furnished with a small spherical adhesive pad at their tips. This species is one of the few to possess a fovea in the eye that enables it to see the smallest details. As it is more diurnal than nocturnal, its

Sphaerodactylus savagei, a fairly typical small reef gecko. Notice the rather long and pointed snout and the white bands on the tail, features that help identify the species. Photo by Robert S. Simmons.

Sphaerodactylus notatus notatus, a reef gecko. This specimen was taken in the Florida Keys. Scientists are still divided as to whether Florida populations of reef geckos are native or were established from ships beaching on the Keys over the last 200 years. Photo by R. T. Zappalorti.

pupils are only slightly elliptical, almost round. The ground color varies from reddish brown to gray-brown. Numerous fine white or yellow flecks cover the body. Often, especially on the head, these form into thin lines.

BIOLOGY, CARE, AND BREEDING: This and other species in the subfamily are ideal for keeping and breeding in the terrarium. They are best kept in small all-glass terraria (length from 30 cm) with adequate ventilation. The substrate should consist of a mixture of sand and potting compost. Furnishings include a couple of bizarre roots or branches that will increase the climbing area and provide hiding places. A couple of creeping plants such as *Scindapsus aureus* or *Tradescantia* will decorate the terrarium and help to maintain the humidity. The interior should be sprayed lightly every day so the animals can drink the droplets. The humidity should not fall below 50%, otherwise skin problems may develop that would be fatal to the geckos. Lighting should be maintained for 12–14 hours per day. A range of temperature

The juvenile *Sphaerodactylus elegans* is beautifully marked, but unfortunately the colors and pattern fade in the adult. This species also occurs in Florida, where it probably is introduced. Photo by Robert S. Simmons.

from 20–32°C should be maintained during the day, but at night this may stay around 20°C. Given these conditions, the geckos will feed, remain healthy, and become active by day. Apart from the usual food insects, a large amount of *Drosophila* may be given.

Sphaerodactylus cinereus, like other members of the subfamily, reproduces with a single egg per clutch, but there may be up to six clutches per year. The eggs are hard-shelled and oval, about 6–8 mm long, and weigh 0.13–0.19 g. They may be buried or deposited in bark crevices. With a relative humidity of 50–60% and an incubation temperature of 26–30°C, the 30–32 mm young will hatch in

67–95 days. They are colored differently from the adults. The head is light blue-green, the body yellowish brown, and the tail orange to red. Black transverse bands run from the tip of the snout to about half way along the tail.

Juveniles are easy to rear in the conditions described above and may be fed on fruitflies, small crickets, etc. Vitamin and mineral supplements should also be provided.

Other *Sphaerodactylus* species can be kept and bred in the same way as *S. cinereus*, but the humidity must match that of the particular wild habitat.

Gonatodes vittatus
Striped Gecko

RANGE: Northern South America, including Colombia, Venezuela, and the islands of Aruba, Margarita, Coche, Cubagua, Los Frailes, Los Testigos, Tobago, Trinidad, and possibly on the island of Curacao.

HABITAT: This species lives on trees but is not averse to living near human habitations. It may therefore be seen in garden trees and even on flower bed borders.

DESCRIPTION: Many *Gonatodes* species are attractively colored and have recently increased in popularity as terrarium subjects.

The Yellow-headed Gecko, *Gonatodes albogularis*, varies considerably over its Caribbean range and often differs greatly from individual to individual. This is a male of the subspecies *fuscus*, probably not in breeding condition. Photo by J. T. Collins.

Some *Gonatodes* can compete with *Phelsuma* in brilliance of color.

As with other *Gonatodes* species, *G. vittatus* shows a marked sexual dimorphism in color and markings. The male has a black-bordered white longitudinal stripe running from the snout along the spine to the tip of the tail. The ground color is ocher, and the flanks are gray. The throat can be white, black and white, or golden yellow. On the upper side of the forelimbs is a black-bordered white patch. The female is plain brown, gray, or khaki colored with dark brown and white flecks; a light back stripe is barely discernible.

The body and tail are round in section and, like the head, are covered with tiny granular scales. There is a narrow row of adhesive lamellae under each toe. The toes are narrow, and each possesses a strong claw. The Striped Gecko reaches a length of 70–85 mm (sometimes even 100 mm), of which roughly half is the tail.

BIOLOGY, CARE, AND BREEDING: In addition to the advantage of its attractive coloration, this species

An exquisitely marked male *Gonatodes humeralis* from Peru. Males of many *Gonatodes* are truly beautiful, if small, lizards. Photo by Paul Freed.

Two males in full color of *Gonatodes albogularis*. The differences in head pattern (note especially the gray stripe behind the eye in the male below) may be due to subspecific or individual variation. Photo above by Robert S. Simmons, that below by Kenneth T. Nemuras.

This male *Gonatodes ceciliae* is a striking lizard even though only a few centimeters long. Notice the similarity in markings and color to the male *Gonatodes humeralis* illustrated earlier. The specific characters of most *Gonatodes* are variations on a basic plan, making their identification difficult. Photo by J. D. Hardy, Jr.

Facing page: Two more views of *Gonatodes albogularis* males. The Yellow-headed Gecko is a truly beautiful lizard that is not hard to maintain and often appears in the pet trade. In most cases, only territorial males attain full color, females and non-breeding males being much duller. Photos by Kenneth T. Nemuras.

Non-breeding males of *Gonatodes albogularis*, the upper photo a specimen from Key West, Florida. This is the way the lizards look most of the time, the full color only appearing in some individuals for short periods. Photo above by R. T. Zappalorti, that below by Robert S. Simmons.

is easy to keep and breed in the terrarium. *Gonatodes vittatus* is a diurnal species, which is reflected in its round pupils. A pair can be kept and will breed in a small, humid, planted terrarium (40 x 30 x 30 cm). They are territorial and, like other members of the genus, both male and female dislike members of their own sex in close proximity.

The female lays up to eight clutches of a single hard-shelled egg per year. They are not buried, but are simply dropped in an exposed position. At an incubation temperature of 26–29°C and a relative humidity of 60–70%, the young will hatch in about 70 days. The juveniles are about 32 mm in length, weigh about 0.14 g, and are similar in color to the female. This species is well suited for beginners.

RELATED SPECIES; *Gonatodes humeralis* and *G. albogularis fuscus* (the Yellow-headed Gecko) may be kept and bred under conditions similar to *G. vittatus*. The eggs (10–12 per female per year) of *G. humeralis* take approximately 70 days to develop; those of *G. a. fuscus* (9 per female per year) take 58–72 days.

A newly hatched specimen of the Yellow-headed Gecko, *Gonatodes albogularis*, from Costa Rica. Banded patterns are common in baby *Gonatodes*, the bands gradually disappearing with maturity as the body becomes more uniform in color. Photo by Paul Freed.

This rather strange lizard sometimes is sold as a gecko, but it actually is *Lepidophyma flavimaculatum*, a spiny night lizard, family Xanthusiidae, from Central America. Although the scales are granular as in geckos and there are tubercles on the sides as in the Turkish Gecko, notice the large and rather normal head scales, which are never found in geckos. Night lizards sometimes are considered to be close relatives of the geckos, but some herpetologists consider them to be related to the skinks. Photo by Kenneth T. Nemuras.

INDEX

Measurement Conversion Factors

When you know—	Multiply by—	To find—
Length:		
Millimeters (mm)	0.04	inches (in)
Centimeters (cm)	0.4	inches (in)
Meters (m)	3.3	feet (ft)
Meters (m)	1.1	yards (yd)
Kilometers (km)	0.6	miles (mi)
Inches (in)	2.54	centimeters (cm)
Feet (ft)	30	centimeters (cm)
Yards (yd)	0.9	meters (m)
Miles (mi)	1.6	kilometers (km)
Area:		
Square centimeters (cm^2)	0.16	square inches (sq in)
Square meters (m^2)	1.2	square yards (sq yd)
Square kilometers (km^2)	0.4	square miles (sq mi)
Hectares (ha)	2.5	acres
Square inches (sq in)	6.5	square centimeters (cm^2)
Square feet (sq ft)	0.09	square meters (m^2)
Square yards (sq yd)	0.8	square meters (m^2)
Square miles (sq mi)	1.2	square kilometers (km^2)
Acres	0.4	hectares (ha)
Mass (Weight):		
Grams (g)	0.035	ounces (oz)
Kilograms (kg)	2.2	pounds (lb)
Ounces (oz)	28	grams (g)
Pounds (lb)	0.45	kilograms (kg)
Volume:		
Milliliters (ml)	0.03	fluid ounces (fl oz)
Liters (L)	2.1	pints (pt)
Liters (L)	1.06	quarts (qt)
Liters (L)	0.26	U.S. gallons (gal)
Liters (L)	0.22	Imperial gallons (gal)
Cubic centimeters (cc)	16.387	cubic inches (cu in)
Cubic meters (cm^3)	35	cubic feet (cu ft)
Cubic meters (cm^3)	1.3	cubic yards (cu yd)
Teaspoons (tsp)	5	millimeters (ml)
Tablespoons (tbsp)	15	millimeters (ml)
Fluid ounces (fl oz)	30	millimeters (ml)
Cups (c)	0.24	liters (L)
Pints (pt)	0.47	liters (L)
Quarts (qt)	0.95	liters (L)
U.S. gallons (gal)	3.8	liters (L)
U.S. gallons (gal)	231	cubic inches (cu in)
Imperial gallons (gal)	4.5	liters (L)
Imperial gallons (gal)	277.42	cubic inches (cu in)
Cubic inches (cu in)	0.061	cubic centimeters (cc)
Cubic feet (cu ft)	0.028	cubic meters (m^3)
Cubic yards (cu yd)	0.76	cubic meters (m^3)
Temperature:		
Celsius (°C)	multiply by 1.8, add 32	Fahrenheit (°F)
Fahrenheit (°F)	subtract 32, multiply by 0.555	Celsius (°C)

Coleonyx (formerly *Anarbylus*) *switaki* of Baja California and Southern California. Photo by K.H. Switak.

TS-166

Keeping and Breeding
GECKOS

Hermann Seufer